Mental Health and Wellbeing

AGYAJIT SINGH
Former Head, Department of Psychology
Punjabi University, Patiala
and
Ex. Sports Psychologist
Netaji Subhas National Institute of Sports, Patiala (Punjab)

PHI Learning Private Limited
Delhi-110092
2026

In fond memory of ***Shri Asoke K. Ghosh*** *(October 1942 – February 2024), Founder Chairman and Managing Director of PHI Learning, whose vision endlessly inspires.*

The Legacy Continues....

Published by Pushpita Ghosh, PHI Learning Private Limited, Rimjhim House, 111, Patparganj Industrial Estate, Delhi-110092 and Printed by Syndicate Binders, A-20, Hosiery Complex, Noida, Phase-II Extension, Noida-201305 (N.C.R. Delhi).

₹ 450.00

MENTAL HEALTH AND WELLBEING
AGYAJIT SINGH

ISBN-978-93-5443-702-1 (Print Book)
ISBN-978-93-5443-996-4 (e-Book)

Dedicated

to

Er. H.S. Sahai

Mr. H.S. Sahai is the most accomplished and contented man who rose from the post of SDO (Electricity) to the highest post of Member Technical in PSEB (now called Punjab State Power Corporation Ltd.) in his lifetime. He is a man with honesty of purpose, dedication, piety, honesty, and believes in hard work. He is my guide, philosopher, and mentor.

CONTENTS

Professor Jitendra Mohan
Professor Emeritus of Psychology

**PANJAB UNIVERSITY,
CHANDIGARH-160014 (INDIA)
MOBILE: +91-9876491321
E-MAIL: jitendramohan74@gmail.com**

FOREWORD

In a period of uncertainty and unparalleled urge to excel, a special book on *Mental Health and Wellbeing* by a distinguished scholar and practitioner is most welcome. Professor Agyajit Singh has lived a life of dedication and passion in terms of Education, Psychology, and Sports. I believe some spiritual energy has been directing him to have published almost One Hundred Books in his lifetime, so far. I am confident that his next book will be in the field of spiritual health and human healing.

I have known him since 1966 and have remained happily surprised by the way he carries on his personal and professional journey with honesty and dignity.

The present book certainly meets the expectations of the young students and teachers to provide understanding and guidance for their improvement and adjustment. I wish the readers enjoy as well as use the ideas and principles for a better society.

Hope, energy, and service will be the outcome of this project.

Jitendra Mohan
President: Asia-Pacific Association of Psychology
Former President: International Society of Mental Training for Excellence
Editor-in-Chief: Indian Journal of Psychology
Professor Emeritus of Psychology Panjab University
Chandigarh
INDIA +91-98764-91321
jitendramohan74@gmail.com

**PRESIDENT: ASIA PACIFIC ACADEMY OF PSYCHOLOGY
MEMBER: INDIAN COUNCIL OF SOCIAL SCIENCE RESEARCH
PRESIDENT: ASIAN CENTRE OF EXCELLENCE
EDITOR-IN-CHIEF: INDIAN JOURNAL OF PSYCHOLOGY
EDITOR-IN-CHIEF: ASIAN JOURNAL OF PSYCHOLOGY & EDUCATION**

PREFACE

The issue of mental health has attracted the attention of psychologists at the beginning of the twenty-first century. Because every tenth person at the global level has become a victim of some kind of mental disorder in this digital age. Psychological well-being is required for everybody to make a person happy, healthy, and prosperous, so that he may lead a long and tension-free life. Psychological well-being consists of mental, emotional, and social health and wellness. Hence, psychological well-being is very much related to mental health. Besides physical health, mental health is also essential to lead a life free from any illness, both physical and psychological. Understanding mental health with psychological well-being is an utmost necessity for every individual. Hence, this book attempts to give knowledge regarding different aspects of mental and emotional health.

The present book, entitled *Mental Health and Wellbeing*, fulfills this purpose. It consists of 12 topics covering different areas of mental health. The first two chapters deal with the concept and nature of mental health and mental hygiene. The next two chapters are related to psychological well-being and human wellness. Emotional health and social health have been discussed in the subsequent chapters. The role of positive behaviour and positive thinking has been elaborately discussed. The problems of mental health are described in the following chapter. Mental health has also been associated in context with mental disorders, frustration, and conflicts. The problem of suicide is also discussed in detail, and lastly, descriptions regarding care, prevention, and promotion of mental and emotional health have found space in this book.

It is hoped that all types of readers, i.e., students, research scholars, professionals, and common people, would like to read this book, because the contents given in this book touch upon their personal lives, and they would like to know the techniques to enhance their mental and emotional health. An attempt has been made to write this book in easy, simple, and understandable language so that every reader may be able to comprehend the material given in the book.

Acknowledgements

The author feels obliged to his students and friends, who are a source of strength and inspiration. He is thankful to his wife, who provided him with all the facilities while writing this book. He expresses her appreciation to Dr. Ramneet Kaur, Assistant Professor at Columbus State University, Georgia in USA, for providing feedback and suggesting improvement in the book. There may be some drawbacks and limitations in this book that will be improved in the next edition of the book. For that, constructive analysis and positive feedback would be welcomed from the readers.

With best wishes, this book is dedicated to esteemed readers.

Dr. AGYAJIT SINGH

1

MENTAL HEALTH—NATURE AND CONCEPT

INTRODUCTION

Mental Health is a state of mental functioning that goes by societal norms and standards, and according to the existing environment of that person. Just as physical health is essential, mental health has also been necessary these days of turmoil. Whereas physical health means that a person is physically fit to lead an ordinary life, or it means the absence of any physical diseases, similarly, mental health means that a person is not only mentally fit but also away from any mental disorders. Adjustment is life, so if a person is well-adjusted in his personal, social, and professional life, he has good mental health.

Mental health refers to cognitive, affective, and conative well-being. It is all about how we think, feel, and behave. So Mental health is an integral and essential component of total health. The World Health Organization (2005) states: "Health is a state of complete physical, mental, and social well-being and not merely the absence of disease or infirmity." Mental health is a state of psychological well-being where a person realizes his potential and achieves the goals set by him. Moreover, he can cope with the strains and stress of life and can work efficiently and contribute to his society. Hence, individuals must be able to maintain their physical and mental health to earn a living and enjoy life. In this chapter, we will discuss the concept and importance of mental health in our ordinary lives.

CONCEPT OF MENTAL HEALTH

Total health status means that a person should be physically fit, mentally alert, emotionally mature, and socially adjusted. So, the modern concept of health is concerned with physical, mental, emotional, and social health. This concept of health extends beyond the proper functioning of the body. It includes a sound, efficient mind and controlled emotions. It means that both body and mind are working efficiently and harmoniously. Mental health is defined as positive mood, general well-being, and being relatively free from the symptoms of anxiety and depression.

A physically healthy individual is less vulnerable to physical illnesses and is better able to confront psychological strains and stresses. So good physical health leads to good mental health. But health these days is not only confined to physical health. It also consists of the mental and emotional health of a person. Mental health does not mean the absence of mental illness, but it is the overall general well-being and wellness of an individual. A mentally healthy person should be stress-free, be able to cope with the hustle and bustle of life and tolerate the frustration of modern life. He will lead a life with fewer needs and face fewer problems. He should not face any stress or anxiety, or mental conflict, and if he does, he should be able to resolve it as early as possible. He should have positive thinking, a positive attitude towards life; have harmonious and cordial relationships with others in his neighborhood, including his family members, friends, peer-mates, and colleagues at his workplace. He must be able to adjust to his environment and be happy even in odd hours.

MEANING OF MENTAL HEALTH

According to the World Health Report (2001), "Mental health is defined as the successful performance of mental functions which result in productive activities, fulfilling relationships with other people, and the capacity to adjust to change and cope with difficulties and hardships." The World Health Organization defines mental health as "a state of wellness in which the individual realizes his or her abilities, can cope with the normal stresses of life, can work productively and fruitfully, and can contribute to his or her community" (WHO, 2005). The WHO contends that mental health is "more than just the absence of mental disorders or disabilities."

According to Hadfield," Mental health is the full and harmonious functioning of the whole personality." It is the positive and active quality of the individual's daily living. It means the ability to balance feelings, desires, ambitions, and ideals that are daily working in one's life, as well as the ability to face and accept the realities of life. It means that thoughts, feelings, and actions function harmoniously toward a common end. His attitudes towards life and habits of work should bring maximum satisfaction and happiness to the individual. So, it consists of three aspects: i.e., (i) full expression, (ii) harmonization, and (iii) the common end.

Mental health is described as either a level of psychological well-being or an absence of mental disorder (WHO 2005). From the perspective of the discipline of positive psychology, mental health may include an individual's ability to enjoy life and procure a balance between life activities and efforts to achieve psychological resilience. "Mental health is an expression of positive emotions and signifies a successful adaptation to a range of demands." (World Health Report, 2001). Recently, the field of Global Mental Health has emerged, which has defined mental health as "the area of study, research, and practice that places a priority on improving mental health and achieving equity in mental health for all people worldwide" (Patel & Prince, 2010).

Mental health and psychological well-being are interrelated, as both terms indicate the same connotation. Psychological well-being shows the wellness of oneself as well as other people, as the individual must function in society and seek his ordinary needs and demands of everyday life. But mental health is a relative state of mind when he is facing the rigors of life and stressful life events. Moreover, he is to adjust to his immediate environment. Although the terms are often used interchangeably. Mental health is a state of emotional and psychological well-being, in which an individual can use his or her cognitive and emotional capabilities, so that he or she can function in society.

Mental health refers to such abilities as making decisions, problem-solving, and assuming responsibilities according to one's capabilities and capacities, finding personal satisfaction, feeling success, and happiness in the accomplishment of everyday tasks, and living effectively with others. A mentally healthy individual understands his motives and desires, his weaknesses, and his strong points. He has developed a lifestyle that gives meaning and honesty of purpose to his daily activities. Such a person has developed a capacity to tolerate frustration and disappointments in his daily life. He shows emotional maturity in his behaviour. He has a wide variety of interests and diverse likings and dislikes and generally lives a well-balanced life both at home and at his place of work.

Basically, Mental health has both individual and social aspects. The individual aspect shows that the individual is internally adjusted. He is self-confident, self-reliant, self-sufficient, adequate, and free from internal conflicts and tensions. He can adapt himself to novel situations. The social aspect indicates that the individual must adjust to society's value systems, customs, traditions, and cultural patterns that promote the general welfare of the individuals. It is within this social framework that internal adjustment must be made. As such, mental health is a process of social adjustment, which involves adaptation and compromise.

Hence, mental health has been defined as the ability of the individual to make personal and social adjustments. If he can make a satisfactory relationship between himself and his environment, between his needs, desires, and those of other people, or if he can meet the demands of a situation, then it means that he has achieved adjustment. Adjustment results in happiness, which implies that emotional conflicts and tension have been resolved.

Mental health can be seen as a continuum, whereas on one side, an individual's mental health may have many different norms and values. Mental wellness is generally viewed as a positive attribute, such that a person can reach enhanced levels of mental health, even if the person does not have any diagnosed mental health condition. On the other side of the continuum, poor mental health and mental illness are not on the same scale. A person can experience poor mental health and not be diagnosed with a mental illness. Likewise, a person diagnosed with a mental illness can experience periods of physical, mental, and social wellness. This definition of mental health highlights emotional well-being, the capacity to live a full and creative life, and the flexibility to deal with life's inevitable challenges.

Mental health can also be defined as the absence of a major mental health condition. Mental health is more than the mere absence of any mental disorder or illness. Quite simply, mental health refers to a person's mental health of the mind and its functioning. Therefore, the impact of social, cultural, physical, and educational factors can all affect someone's mental health.

DIFFERENT VIEWPOINTS OF MENTAL HEALTH

There are various viewpoints regarding the concept of mental health, which are given below:

1. **Mental wellness**: Mental wellness is generally considered a positive characteristic, which allows a person to reach enhanced levels of mental health, even if the person has not been diagnosed with a mental health condition. This definition of mental health highlights mental wellness, which gives the capacity to live a full and creative life and has the flexibility to deal with life's inevitable challenges. Many therapeutic strategies and techniques have offered methods that are proven to be effective and proactive for further improving the mental wellness of healthy people. Positive psychology places much emphasis on mental health.

   An example of a mental wellness model includes one developed by Myers, Sweeney, and Witmer. It includes five life tasks—(i) Essence or spirituality, (ii) Work and leisure, (iii) Friendship, (iv) Love, and (v) Self-direction—and twelve sub-tasks— (i) sense of worth, (ii) sense of control, (iii) realistic beliefs, (iv) emotional awareness, and coping, (v) problem solving and creativity, (vi) sense of humor, (vii) nutrition, (viii) exercise, (ix) self-care, (x) stress management, (xi) gender identity, and (xii) cultural identity—which are identified as characteristics of healthy functioning and a major component of wellness (Myers, Sweeny, & Witmer, 2000).

2. **Lack of a mental disorder:** Mental health has also been defined as the absence of a major mental health condition (for example, a condition diagnosed in the DSM-IV), though recent evidence suggests that mental health is more than the mere absence of a mental disorder or illness. Simply, mental health refers to a person's mental functioning of the mind (Barbara Kozier, 2008). Research has shown that there is a stigma attached to mental illness. Although the term mental health is commonly used, many doctors say that bad mental health leads to some psychological disorders that have their origin in physical diseases.
3. **Cultural and religious considerations:** Mental health is a socially defined concept, i.e., different societies, groups, cultures, institutions, and professions have very different ways of describing its nature and causes, determining what is mentally healthy, and deciding what interventions, if any, are appropriate (Weare, Katherine, 2000). Thus, different professional experts will have different cultural, class, political, and religious backgrounds, impacting the methodology applied during treatment.

MENTAL HEALTH Vs. TOTAL HEALTH

Mental health or wellness is based on total health/fitness. Physical fitness is usually considered the fitness of the body, but in the modern concept, total fitness means fitness of both body and mind due to the dual relationship of body and mind. Physical fitness is one aspect of total fitness. Total fitness or health is considered the capacity and capabilities of a person to function in everyday life at his best.

A new concept of total health includes mental, emotional, and social as well as physical health. Thus, when total health is used in its modern terms, it includes the physical, mental, emotional, and social components. All these components play a significant role in leading a full and happy life. "Freedom from disease, organic development, efficient movement, alertness of mind, emotional maturity, and social adjustment provide the framework of total fitness and health. It has been said that fitness not only adds years to one's life but life to one's years. Thus, fitness is not a state for the young; it is for all ages" (Barrow, 1977).

Frost (1971) says that fitness "is the capacity of the individual to live and function effectively, purposefully and zestfully and to meet confidently the problems and crises which are among life's expectations." A fit person is free from diseases or the absence of any illness and possesses adequate strength and endurance, agility, and skill to live a productive and happy life. He is zestful, vital, and energetic in terms of his abilities, capacities, and other characteristics. He is well integrated and rational and has the will to act, to think, and behave properly. He is heading towards self-fulfilment, self-realization, and self-actualization.

Total fitness and health would imply that the individual must exhibit social adjustability, emotional maturity, mental efficiency, and perhaps even positive, moral, and spiritual qualities. If a society is to remain strong physically, mentally, spiritually, and socially, there must be an emphasis on total fitness. Fitness is the ability of a person to live a full and balanced life.

The healthy person possesses physical well-being and qualities such as good human relations, maturity, and high ethical values. He also fulfills such basic needs as love, affection, recognition, security, and self-respect. According to this view, the general pattern of an individual's total fitness is his personality and the different characteristics. A man's personality is the total picture of his whole behaviour. For the development of the personality of an individual, he must be physically fit, mentally alert, emotionally mature, and socially adjusted. The mental, emotional, and social development depends on the sound foundation of physical development, which is based on physical fitness.

The American Association for Health, Physical Education and Recreation (AAHPER, 1963) defines total fitness as "that state which characterizes the degree to which the person can function. Fitness is an individual matter. It implies the ability of each person to live most effectively with his potential. The ability to function depends upon the physical, mental, emotional, social, and spiritual components of fitness, all of which are related to each other and are mutually interdependent.

Total health also includes the mental health of an individual. If a person wants to be mentally healthy, firstly, he should be a physically healthy and physically fit person. To keep oneself physically fit, one should be considerate regarding one's diet and nutrition. Food and intake are very important elements in our physical health. Secondly, we should continue with morning walks and physical exercises after the walk, which will lead to total fitness. Moreover, you should also concentrate on your sleeping patterns. About seven to eight hours of sleep is essential for an ordinary person. Try to shun beverages and alcohol in your lifestyle. Smoking should also be avoided if you want to live a long life. In this way, you can remain a physically fit and healthy person. And if you are physically healthy, it is undeniable that you will also be mentally healthy.

NEED FOR AND IMPORTANCE OF MENTAL HEALTH

These days, mental health is more important than physical health, as mental disorders are increasing day by day. Therefore, mental health is essential for every individual in today's modern life, where life has become faster and more complex. We are all concerned with the issues regarding mental health these days. Mental health refers to a stress-free life, no anxiety, and the absence of any depressive disorders.

Maintaining good mental health is required for a long and healthy life. Good mental health can enhance the quality of life, but if bad, it can minimize the happiness of living a normal life. For this, emotional support is essential for mental health. With the help of emotional and social support, your mental health can improve and prevent mental disorders. A support system is an asset, and those who do not have social and emotional support are likely to develop mental disorders. This emotional, social, and moral support from your friends and relatives can lead to an increase in personal competence, commitment, control, and challenges in life. It will also lead to a sense of stability and recognition of self-worth and can have a positive effect on quality of life.

Mental health indicates our psychological well-being, which consists of emotional, psychological, and social wellness. It affects our cognitive, affective, and conative domains of behaviour. It helps us understand how we handle stress, communicate with others, and make healthy responses. Mental health is important at every stage of life, from childhood and adolescence through adulthood.

Mental health is also an important component of total health. For example, mental disorders like depression increase the risk of many types of physical health problems, particularly diabetes, heart disease, and brain stroke. Similarly, the presence of chronic disease can increase the risk of mental illness and disorders. So mental health is as important as it can affect our physical health.

Mental health can affect our daily lives and personal relationships. Moreover, mental health can help a person enjoy his daily life. It helps in achieving a balance between different activities in daily life. It tries to integrate and coordinate life activities, responsibilities, and efforts to reach psychological resilience. Mental conditions such as stress, anxiety, and depression can all affect mental health adversely and disrupt a person's routine life.

Many factors in people's lives affect interpersonal relationships, but physical factors can contribute to mental health maintenance. It is important to know that mental health depends on several factors and many elements of life. Multiple factors, like physical, social, and psychological, determine the level of mental health of a person. For example, anger, violence, and aggression are recognized as risk factors to mental health, especially associated with sexual violence.

With the advancement of scientific investigation and technological innovations, enough work has been done for the development of our country, whereas diseases, poverty, and other problems that have plagued our society in the past have been eradicated. But the strains of modern life have increased tension, so that one out of every ten people in society has become a victim of mental diseases. This problem has raised the need for maintenance of mental health.

The National Association for Mental Health estimates that one out of every two patients seeking medical aid is suffering from an illness related to mental and emotional disorders. This does not necessarily mean that the complaints of such people are imaginary. But it simply means that mental or emotional difficulties in some ways have contributed to the patient's illness. Hence, there is a need to start a program of mental health care in our society on a large scale. The importance of mental health can be assessed from the following points:

1. A mentally healthy person is a social one because he obeys the laws and customs of the community in which he lives and through which he finds the fullest development and satisfaction of his personality and fulfills his needs and demands.
2. Mental health is described at cognitive or affective levels of well-being, which shows an absence of a mental disorder. Mental health may include an individual's ability to enjoy life and seek a balance between life activities and efforts to achieve psychological resilience.
3. Mental health is a state of emotional and psychological well-being in which an individual can use his or her cognitive and affective capabilities, function in society, and meet the needs and demands of everyday life. It is related to the achievement and maintenance of psychological well-being. Mental health is a relative state of mind in which a person can cope with the recurrent stresses of everyday living in a socially acceptable way.
4. Mental health includes the way you feel about yourself, the quality of your relationships, and your ability to manage your feelings and deal with difficulties.
5. Mental health is not just the absence of mental health problems. Rather than the absence of mental illness, mental health refers to the presence of positive characteristics. While some people may not have negative feelings, they still need to engage in activities that promote positive feelings to achieve mental and emotional well-being.

To sum up, it can be said that mental health is important because it can help us in many ways. These points are given in the following box:

CHARACTERISTICS OF MENTAL HEALTH
1. Coping with the strains and stresses of life
2. Remain physically healthy and physically fit
3. Have good interpersonal relationships
4. Make meaningful contributions to your community and society
5. Work productively and efficiently
6. Realize your full potential and dreams.

FACTORS OF MENTAL HEALTH

There are some significant factors on which the mental health of any individual depends:

- Heredity factors
- Physical factors
- Social factors
- Satisfaction with fundamental needs

1. **Heredity or Biological factors:** These factors provide raw material for the potential of the individual. They set the foundation for his mental health. The individual inherits potentialities of physical appearance, abilities, etc., from his parents. The development of these potentialities is basically determined by genetic factors and environmental influences. In some mental disorders, like psychoneurosis and psychosis trends, hereditary factors play an important role. Heredity supplies a predisposing trend for personality maladjustments.

2. **Physical factors:** Physical factors make a significant contribution to mental health, i.e., erect posture like height and weight, colors of the skin, and inculcate a smiling face, feeling of exhilaration, mood, and a sense of security. Physical health has an important role in the development of personality characteristics. An individual with feelings of physical fitness has a good mental disposition and is mentally alert. He has a great desire to live, to achieve, and to be successful. Physical health increases motivation, drive, and the motive to achieve happiness in life.

3. **Social factors:** The social factors are concerned with the individual's relationship with society in which he lives, as well as the interactional processes and social functioning with other people. The social environment provides the individual with the knowledge, skills, interests, attitudes, habits, values, and goals that he acquires. Home and school influence his behaviour. He inculcates a sense of personal worth, social awareness, and social competency. The community provides the environment within the family and neighborhood. A healthy atmosphere in society enhances the feelings of belonging and the opportunities for group participation.

4. **Satisfaction with fundamental needs:** The physical needs, like hunger, thirst, fatigue, lack of sleep, physical pain, exercise, heat or cold, etc., are to be satisfied to maintain physical well-being. Secondary needs should also be satisfied. The secondary needs are love, affection, recognition, achievement, a sense of mental security, and belongingness, etc. The secondary needs are given in the following box:

SECONDARY NEEDS

(a) The ego needs to maintain the self;
(b) Need for a sense of security through love and affection, understanding, trust, cooperation, and overt affection;
(c) Need for recognition or regard as a person of worth and importance;
(d) A feeling of self-enhancement and a sense of adequacy;
(e) Need to grow independently;
(f) Need to play; and
(g) Need to belong to a group.

CHARACTERISTICS OF MENTAL HEALTH

Based on the factors mentioned above, the characteristics of mental health can be described as follows:

1. **Physical and intellectual development:** Physical and intellectual development are two very important aspects for maintaining mental health. We cannot say that mental health can be maintained without considering our physical health, as both body and mind are related to each other. If somebody keeps good physical health, then he will also be mentally healthy. Similarly, a person who is not mentally healthy will not be physically fit.

2. **Emotional and social development:** Emotional and social development are also necessary for the development of the personality of an individual, as well as mental health, which is an important component of the total health of a person. An integrated personality means that a person should be physically fit, mentally alert, emotionally stable, and socially adjusted. So, an attempt should be made to improve the development of the emotional and social aspects of behaviour.

3. **Development of interests and aptitudes:** For maintaining and promoting mental health, a person should have varied interests and try to fulfill them. Without having any interest in life, life would be dull and drudgery and may cause any mental illness.

So, one should be busy achieving one's goals through his interests. Similarly, every man has aptitudes in some area or other, which is the inborn ability to achieve something in life. Aptitude is your potential, which you may inherit from your parents through genes. If you do not perform based on aptitude, it may lead to mental misery and poor mental health.

4. **Feelings of personal worth, security, and self-confidence:** It is related to the ego strength of an individual. One must have feelings of self-worth, self-assurance, self-prestige, and self-esteem. It will help you to keep balance in your feelings, thinking, and actions, and give you a healthy mental life. The feelings of personal worth further increase your sense of security, which is the social and secondary need of an individual. In this way, your level of self-confidence and self-efficacy will also be enhanced. Without self-confidence, you cannot achieve anything. Hence, personal worth, security, and self-confidence are essential parts of one's mental health.
5. **Understanding of self and others:** You must know thyself. You should know your strengths and weaknesses. It will enhance your self-esteem and self-prestige. In the same way, you should try to understand others to adjust to them. You should try to know their psychological and emotional life, so that you may get along with them and have a harmonious relationship with them.
6. **Understanding of environment for mental health:** The environment is of two types: physical and social environment. The social environment is the type of people surrounding you. Your friends, peer-mates, age-mates, and members of the family—all comprise your social environment. The relationships with them and the interactions that you are making will determine how conducive your social environment is. The better your environment, the better your mental health will be.
7. **Participation in constructive and creative activities:** If you want to lead a healthy and happy life and if you want to be mentally and emotionally healthy, you must participate in leisure-time activities and keep yourself involved in some hobbies. If you take part in some creative activities, you will be able to maintain your good mental health.

All the above characteristics of mental health are given in the following box:

CHARACTERISTICS OF MENTAL HEALTH
1. Adequate physical and intellectual development. 2. Adequate emotional and social development. 3. Adequate development of interests and aptitudes. 4. Adequate feelings of personal worth, security, and self-confidence. 5. Adequate understanding of self and others. 6. Adequate understanding of the environment for mental health. 7. Adequate participation in constructive and creative activities.

These positive characteristics of mental health allow you to fully participate in life through productive thinking and actions, as well as meaningful activities and strong relationships. These positive characteristics also help you cope when faced with life's challenges and stresses.

CHARACTERISTICS OF A MENTALLY HEALTHY PERSON

After discussing the characteristics of mental health, we should know what the characteristics of a mentally healthy person are, as mentally healthy people are required in our society who can contribute something according to their individuality for the development of our society. A mentally healthy person should possess the following characteristics:

1. **Self-knowledge:** A mentally healthy person must know thyself. He should know his strengths and limitations or weaknesses. He should select his various activities in life according to his ability, capacity, and capabilities. A person should have an awareness of his needs, motives, desires, ambitions, and feelings, etc. He should have a full understanding of his behaviour and emotions. He can appraise his assets and liabilities realistically.
2. **Self-esteem:** It consists of the feelings one has about oneself and one's ability to function effectively in society. A mentally healthy person does not have feelings of an inferiority complex or lack of self-confidence. He does not degrade himself but feels a sense of adequacy and can face most of the challenging situations that arise in day-to-day living.
3. **Feelings of security:** A mentally healthy person feels that he is the most honored person in society. He interacts with other people comfortably, reacts independently, and acts with full freedom in different social situations. He wants to be recognized by others, which may lead to independence of action. He has a feeling of personal security. He tries to contribute to the group activities with a positive attitude.

4. **Ability to accept and give affection:** A mentally healthy person can build cordial and affectionate relationships with other people. He has respect for the needs and feelings of others. He does not make unrealistic and unwanted demands upon others for the gratification of his own needs. He can reciprocate the feelings of others and has a feeling of empathy.
5. **Positive philosophy of life:** Such a person has a different lifestyle and has his own philosophy of life, which provides meaningful purposes in his daily work. He works hard, realistically, to solve his problems while living in his society. He does not behave irresponsibly in any type of social functioning. Such a person has a positive life philosophy and can make quick decisions in life. He makes correct decisions after considering all the aspects of the problem explicitly.
6. **Ability to be productive and happy:** A mentally healthy person is generally productive and happy. He can use his abilities and potential in productive activities in relation to other people. He enters his work with a certain amount of zest and enthusiasm.
7. **Absence of tension and hypersensitivity:** A maladjusted person suffers stress, anxiety, and tension. He is hypersensitive to both pleasant and unpleasant aspects of living. He is completely disturbed and upset, even over minor frustration. On the other hand, a mentally healthy person is free from such symptoms.
8. **Control over emotions: A** mentally healthy person is emotionally mature and stable. It means that he can control his emotions like fear, anger, jealousy, etc. He is emotionally balanced and free from any emotional stress. He leads a tension-free life. He can easily manage any stress in life if it occurs.
9. **Self-confidence:** Self-confidence is a good sign of mental health. A mentally healthy person achieves success in every activity through his ability and his self-confidence. He has confidence that he will be able to accomplish the task adequately. Mostly, he can find solutions to problems with his effort and honesty of purpose.
10. **Social adjustment:** A mentally healthy person has the ability and skill to adjust to changing situations. Due to this skill, he can take part in social activities very effectively. He has full assurance and a sense of tolerance. He can solve the difficulties in life rightly, can tolerate the failures, and does not feel frustrated. In fact, he learns from his failures.

A mentally healthy person may be correctly defined as an individual whose all potentialities, whether innate or acquired, are fully developed and harmonized with one another by being directed to a common goal.

It is believed that a mentally healthy person will be efficient and effective socially and morally. A person who directs and coordinates his impulses and urges based on certain aims, ideals, and goals in life will certainly be a mentally healthy person.

To sum up, it can be said that mentally healthy people have the following qualities:

1. They can realize their full potential.
2. They can cope with the stresses of life.
3. They work productively.
4. They make meaningful contributions to their communities.

The following box shows the ways to maintain positive mental health:

SIGNS OF POSITIVE MENTAL HEALTH
1. Getting professional help if required
2. Connecting with other people
3. Have a positive attitude
4. Remain physically active
5. A helping attitude for others
6. Getting enough sound sleep
7. Developing coping skills

Key facts regarding mental health are as follows:

(i) Mental health is more than the absence of mental disorders.

(ii) Mental health is an integral part of total health; indeed, there is no health without mental health.

(iii) Mental health is affected by a range of socio-economic, biological, and environmental factors.

Cost-effective public health strategies and interventions exist to preserve, promote, and restore mental health.

CONCLUSION

Mental health is the functioning of mental processes, effectively and efficiently. Mental health includes emotional, psychological, and social wellness. It has cognitive, affective, and conative ramifications. It affects how we think, feel, act, behave, and relate to others. Mental health means the absence of any mental disease, such as anxiety, depression, obsession, schizophrenia, paranoia, etc. Mental health is an integral and essential component of health. Mental health is described as "a state of wellness in which the individual realizes his or her abilities, can cope with the normal stresses of life, can work productively and fruitfully, and can contribute to his or her community".

Mental health also refers to such abilities as making decisions, assuming responsibilities within one's capacities, finding satisfaction, success, and happiness in the accomplishment of everyday tasks, living effectively with others, and showing considerate behaviour. There are various points of view regarding the concept of mental health. Mental health can affect daily living, relationships, and physical health, as well as preserving a person's ability to enjoy life. There are a few basic and significant factors on which the mental health of any individual depends.

2

MENTAL HYGIENE: CONCEPT AND IMPORTANCE

INTRODUCTION

These days, the issues regarding mental health have become very crucial because many people are suffering from some mental disorder. It is true that one in ten people has some psychological difficulties and is leading a miserable life. They are consulting a psychologist, clinical psychologist, or psychiatrist to seek help for solving their mental problems. The professional experts, with the help of counseling, assist them in overcoming their state of agony and misery. Mental disorders are more troublesome than physical illnesses. So, it is essential to understand the nature of those mental disorders and how they are caused. Hence, it is important to know about the principles of mental health and mental hygiene. Mental health and mental hygiene are related to each other. Mental hygiene refers to the cleaning of the mind of negative thoughts. So, in this chapter, we will acquaint the readers with nature and concepts as well as the importance of mental hygiene in our daily lives.

MENTAL HYGIENE

Mental hygiene is the scientific study of maintaining and preserving mental health and preventing mental disorders to help people lead a life to their potential. It includes all methods adopted to promote and preserve mental health: i.e., to save the mentally disturbed persons from mental illness, and help them in coping with stressful life events. The community mental health service is concerned with the movement of mental hygiene. It deals with social problems regarding mental disorders, from drug addiction to suicide prevention. Mental hygiene includes the prevention of mental illness, which includes prenatal and natal care, child-abuse awareness programs, and counseling for crime victims. It also consists of treatment programs including psychotherapy, play therapy, psychodrama, and behavioural medicine. One of the most important objectives is to combat the stigma still attached to mental illness and encourage those affected to seek treatment. All these are covered under the area of mental hygiene.

Mental disorders are mental illnesses that are caused by various factors prevalent in the environment of the individual. These psychological problems may adversely affect the lives of people who are afflicted with some type of mental disorder. It comes under the scope of mental hygiene to study, analyze, and help mentally ill persons in their care, cure, prevention, and rehabilitation of their maladies. So, treatment in the psychiatric clinics and giving the best care and prevention are some of the functions of mental hygiene. So, it is very important to know the concept, role, and functions of mental hygiene in the promotion of mental health.

CONCEPT OF MENTAL HYGIENE

The concept of mental hygiene is not too old. It was Clifford Beers in 1900 who stimulated a movement for better treatment of mentally insane people. In fact, he himself became a victim of some mental disorder. Adolph Meyer was a pioneer in helping Bears to launch this movement, as he suggested that the term mental hygiene be applied to this new movement. In earlier times, this movement was organized for the specific purpose of giving medical and psychiatric assistance to patients in mental hospitals. The aims of this movement were threefold:

1. To change the old belief that mental disorders are incurable and that they carry a stigma of disgrace.
2. To identify and encourage the early recognition and prevention of mental illness.
3. To improve prevailing structural conditions in mental hospitals.

In the initial stage, this movement was started with the specific purpose of giving medical and psychiatric help to patients in general hospitals. But now, the mental hygiene program aims at the establishment of mental health clinics. Today, the mental hygiene movement has shifted its emphasis from that of cure to that of preservation, i.e., prevention of mental diseases and preservation of mental health. It has a two-fold function. Mental hygiene now aims at the establishment of mental hospitals or psychiatric clinics in medical colleges. So, mental hygiene is meant for maintaining and sustaining mental health.

Hadfield, an expert in mental health, considers that mental hygiene is "concerned with the maintenance of mental health and the prevention of mental disorder." According to Crow and Crow (1962), "Mental hygiene is a science that deals with human welfare and pervades all fields of human relationships." They consider that mental hygiene has three major purposes to perform. They are:

(i) the prevention of mental disorder through an understanding of the relationship that exists between wholesome personality development and life experiences.
(ii) the preservation of the mental health of the individual and of the group.
(iii) the discovery and utilization of therapeutic measures to cure mental illness.

Hence, the functions of mental hygiene may be twofold: i.e., (i) the prevention of mental disorders, and (ii) their cure. Mental hygiene is not meant only for those who are mentally ill, but it is also concerned with the normal human beings. It is related to making our lives increasingly useful and worthy. It is concerned with the psychological well-being of everyone. It is an attempt to conserve and promote mental health.

The purpose of the mental hygiene program is the development of well-adjusted personalities. It tries to discover maladjustment in its earliest forms and to overcome them as soon as possible. It provides strategies for bringing those individuals who have developed more serious maladjustments or mental disorders.

Mental Hygiene is one of the branches of psychiatry that deals with the scientific study of maintaining and preserving mental health, and of preventing mental disorders through counselling, early treatment, and educational measures. *Mental hygiene* is the practice of trying to maintain mental health through proactive behaviour and treatment.

Mental health and mental hygiene are correlated. Whereas *mental health is "one's overall psychological well-being,"* mental *hygiene refers to methods for preserving health. In this way, mental hygiene is what you do to keep your mind clean and healthy. Practicing mental hygiene is an ongoing process. Understanding what it is and how to practice it can help improve your lifestyle and quality of life.*

There are some misconceptions regarding the cure and prevention of mental illnesses, which characterized the medical attitude toward mental diseases, contributing to the dissociation of mental medicine and its problems from the subjects that were engaging the attention of physicians. There seemed little likelihood that the determination to prevent diseases, which was beginning to dominate the medical profession, would soon extend into the domain of mental medicine.

CONTRIBUTIONS OF MENTAL HYGIENE

Some misconceptions exist about the prevention and treatment of mental disorders, as some people still believe that it is a God sent evil, and some devil has inflicted that man who is suffering from some insanity. So there seemed to be slow progress in the scientific treatment of mental illnesses. The medical profession first advocates for the prevention of the disease, and later, if it occurs, it thinks of devising some method of treatment for the rehabilitation of the patient. The knowledge that many forms of mental illness depend upon preventable causes has given birth to the rapid growth of psychiatry, a new branch in medicine, and the newly discovered techniques for utilizing its resources in practical attempts to deal with psycho-social problems, which have broken down the barriers that so long and so effectually isolated mental medicine. This is an area of mental hygiene.

The following points throw light on the contribution of mental hygiene:

1. Mental hygiene has contributed much to reducing serious maladjustments and mental disorders through the early recognition of its symptoms. The program of mental hygiene has led to the establishment of clinics, and thus, facilities have been provided for the treatment of mental disorders. Above all, mental hygiene has emphasized that psychologists should have adequate training to remove the causes of frustration and conflicts among people.
2. The most important contribution of mental hygiene is regarding the propagation of the contention that problematic behaviour and mental disorders should be studied scientifically. Moreover, the approach to the maladjusted and abnormal people would be sympathetic and helpful rather than one of blame, disgust, or hate.
3. Mental hygiene aims at the preservation of mental health. Mental health is recognized today as an important aspect of one's total health status. The modern concept of health extends beyond the proper functioning of the body. It also includes a sound, efficient mind and controlled emotions. It means that both body and mind are working efficiently and harmoniously. Mental health is a basic factor that contributes to the maintenance of physical health as well as social effectiveness. Mental hygiene investigates this aspect of mental health.
4. Mental hygiene deals with certain principles and factors of living together that serve as a guide to human adjustments. It includes those life patterns that promote the development of wholesome and socially adjusted personalities. It helps an individual to get along with himself and with his fellow friends, to inculcate desirable attitudes, to avoid conflicts that bring maladjustments, and to develop positive and rational behaviour.

5. Another approach of mental hygiene is a preventive one, which is based on the principle of exposing oneself to environmental influences that will enable each person to develop his full potential, to attain emotional stability, and to achieve personal and social adjustments.

Other functions of mental hygiene are as follows:

1. **Mental hygiene can improve mood, decrease stress:** It has been observed that our mind can benefit from a quick morning routine of walking and jogging, as well as physical exercises. It can improve mood, develop better relationships with others, and even increase deeper concentration and enhance creativity. Mental hygiene programs include simple practices that improve our quality of life by preventing negative behaviours and providing emotional stability. For some people, mental hygiene means dedicating a few minutes of their morning routine to meditation, stretching, or walking.
2. **A focused mind is a happy mind:** Research has shown that concentration of mind is best for our mental health. In fact, attention focuses the mind on one task, whereas concentration is parking your mind at a particular place. For the concentration of the mind, people practice yoga and meditation. It all leads to a happy mind, which is a sign of happiness. This is why paying attention to daily routines can make such a big impact, especially for busy, highly accomplished people. Developing a happy, focused mind helps us be more creative and productive and have better relationships with others.
3. **Building a calm and quiet brain:** Research has suggested that the brain is incredibly adaptable. For example, after eight weeks of a mindfulness-based stress reduction program, practitioners have found decreased activity in the brain structure that is responsible for fear and stress responses. Anyone interested in the concept of mental hygiene should find what works for them by experimenting with bringing mindfulness exercises to different activities.

From early childhood until late life, mental hygiene is considered the springboard of thinking, acting, and feeling, as well as communication skills, learning, emotional growth and development, resilience for recovering quickly, and self-esteem. A person's mental health hygiene is subject to a variety of changes in life, either from genetic causes to environmental stressors, or physiological changes that may occur during their lifetime.

Mental Health Hygiene and Adjustment

Mental health and mental hygiene are closely related to life adjustment, emotional maturity, and a positive attitude towards the social environment.

A man is born with some physiological and psychological needs. He remains busy throughout his life to fulfill his needs, but all his needs are not fulfilled; some of them remain unfulfilled, which creates problems. Then he continues to solve his problems. When he is unable to solve the problems, that puts some pressure on his mind, which results in strain and stress. Stress creates anxiety, which leads to tension in one's life. It is the cause of frustration in life. When our needs are not fulfilled or thwarted, the outcome is frustration, which is quite troublesome in life. You lose your peace of mind, are unable to concentrate on your work, and are unable to perform well. It is all related to the problem of adjustment and maladjustment in life. Our mental health hygiene is concerned with how well we are adjusted to our social environment.

Adjustment is the process of maintaining a balance between the needs and the conditions that affect the satisfaction of these needs. An individual sets the goals and proceeds towards the satisfaction of those needs, but on the way, he encounters many obstacles that block or thwart his activities in the fulfillment of these needs. Either he will have to change the goals or the means to achieve the goals. In this whole process, he tries to adjust himself. This analysis indicates the essential aspects of the adjustment processes.

The process of adjustment starts right from the day of the birth of the child, and it continues throughout his life. The concept of adjustment is very old. This concept originated from Darwin's theory of evolution. He used the term 'adaptation', as it has a biological origin. Man, among the living beings, has the highest capacities to adapt to new situations. As a social animal, he not only adapts to physical demands but also adjusts to social pressures.

Biologists used the term adaptation strictly for physiological demands, but psychologists use the term 'adjustment' for several conditions of social or inter-personal relations in society. Thus, adjustment means a reaction to the demands and pressures of the social environment of the individual. For example, a child has to follow certain beliefs and a set of values that the family follows. His personality develops in the continuous process of interaction with his family environment. If the internal demands, such as hunger, water, oxygen, and sleep, are not fulfilled, he feels uncomfortable. With the development of the child, these physiological demands increase and become more complex.

These two types of demands sometimes come into conflict with each other and subsequently make the adjustment a complicated process for the individual. Conflicts among the various needs or demands of a person present a special problem of adjustment. If you gratify one of the conflicting needs, the need that is not gratified will produce frustration and, sometimes, abnormal behaviour.

Now the term 'adjustment' is used in terms of the personality construct of an individual. The individual acts as a unit, thinking, feeling, working, and is affected by various types of influences in his immediate environment. It is the integration of all characteristics, both physical and mental, learned or unlearned, which constitute his total personality. This is his life adjustment.

There are various types of adjustments shown by different individuals at different times. The techniques of adjustment also vary widely in how they reduce the tensions aroused by a conflicting situation. The best methods of tension reduction are those in which the individual consciously tries to reduce the tension.

The opposite term is maladjustment, which is the lack of adjustment. Everyone in his lifetime faces obstacles and experiences frequent thwarting, failures, and disappointments while achieving his goals, which leads to frustration and conflicts in life. Conflict is the state of instability of mind and the inability to make decisions. Frustration leads to mental health problems. There are adaptive and maladaptive techniques to cope with frustrating situations. Conflicts can also be resolved with a defense mechanism, which is one of the methods of mental hygiene.

Mental health and mental hygiene consist of adjustment, and adjustment is a lifelong process. The essential aspects of adjustment processes involve: (i) the existence of a motive, (ii) circumstances leading to its thwarting, (iii) resulting in varied responses which may eventually lead, (iv) the discovery of a solution.

MENTAL HYGIENE AND EMOTIONAL MATURITY

Emotional maturity is a sign of mental health and mental hygiene. The more mature a person is emotionally, the better his mental health. Researchers have found that there is a positive and high relationship between mental health and emotional maturity. Emotional maturity is related to emotional behaviour. An emotionally mature person can demonstrate stable and well-balanced emotional behaviour in his day-to-day life. Such a person may have in his possession almost all types of emotions, positive or negative, and can express them at the appropriate time and at an appropriate place skilfully in different situations of life.

Mental hygiene refers to the presence of some positive characteristics, and the most important characteristic is emotional maturity. Emotional maturity is an important part of mental hygiene. Emotional maturity is a mental state of balanced behaviour, i.e., thinking, feelings, and self-control. An emotionally stable and mature person will have better adjustment with himself as well as with others. He will have more satisfaction in life and have a positive and balanced attitude towards life. So, emotional maturity refers to proper emotional management and control.

Mental hygiene, which is due to the emotional maturity of an individual, is based on how his emotions have been developed. Emotional development includes the ability to identify, recognize, and understand one's feelings, and comprehend emotional states in oneself and in others, to control strong emotions and their expression constructively, and to establish and maintain relationships.

An emotionally mature person is friendly towards others and is more motivated by pleasure, satisfaction, and contentment. He may not have resolved all situations of hostilities, anxieties, and frustrations. However, he is continuously involved in a struggle to lead a mature, balanced, and healthy emotional life.

Emotional maturity implies managing your emotions in constructive ways. Your emotional maturity depicts your capacity to control your emotions and to evaluate others' emotional states. It is very much influenced by his/her cordial relationship with others. Emotional intelligence plays an important part in one's life in developing emotional maturity.

According to Arthur T. Jersild (1968), "Emotional maturity means the degree to which the person has realized his potential for richness of living and has developed his capacity to enjoy things, to relate himself to others, to love and to laugh; his capacity for whole-hearted sorrow when an occasion for grief arises; his capacity for experiencing anger when faced with thwarting; and his capacity to show fear when there is occasion to be frightened, without feeling a need to use a false mask of courage such as must be assumed by persons afraid to admit that they are afraid."

Alexander Magnum's view regarding emotional maturity is that it is the refined and developed ability to understand and use one's emotions in personally controlled ways. He listed the following signs of emotional maturity, which are given in the following box:

SIGNS OF EMOTIONAL MATURITY

1. Confidence and respect for one's integrity.
2. Ability to face reality honestly.
3. Self-control even in upsetting situations.
4. The desire to serve instead of the desire to shine.
5. Well-developed discrimination.
6. Believing in oneself to be important.
7. Recognizing and evaluating pressure from other people.

Emotional maturity indicates that conditions when a man experiences his feelings for his well-being and develops the ability to derive pleasure from material. It is not only the effective determinant of personality patterns but also helps to control the growth of individual development. The concept of mature emotional behaviour at any level reflects the fruits of normal emotional development. The importance of emotional maturity in life cannot be overemphasized. A truly educated person is one whose emotions are trained and under control.

PRINCIPLES OF MENTAL HYGIENE

Mental hygiene, which is related to mental health, follows the following principles:

1. To know what a person wants and how he will do it to make it happen.
2. It is better to think than act soon and have control over one's behaviour.
3. To develop a sense of self-reliance and the capability to take responsibility for one's life and actions.
4. To have patience in life.
5. To develop the ability to communicate with others cooperatively and positively. Have strong bonds with others in a supportive and constructive manner.
6. To get along with them, genuinely care about others.
7. To act with honesty of purpose and try to live by one's principles.
8. One should have self-control and balance in everything in life.
9. One should have the capacity to tackle difficult and demanding situations.
10. One should have the ability to follow through, even when it is difficult.
11. One should have humility and the ability to say, "I was wrong. I am sorry."

The above-mentioned principles are requisite for every person in this world to keep his mental hygiene effective so that he may lead a comfortable, pleasurable, and enjoyable life. The mature person has developed attitudes about himself and his environment, which have developed his thoughts and behaviour.

CHARACTERISTICS OF MENTAL HYGIENE

Some of the characteristics of mental hygiene are suggested below:

1. To accept criticism gratefully, being honestly glad for an opportunity to improve.
2. Do not indulge in self-pity but begin to feel the laws of compensation operating in all life.
3. Do not expect special consideration from anyone.

4. To control his temper.
5. To face emergencies with poise.
6. Feelings should not be easily hurt.
7. To accept the responsibility of one's actions.
8. To recognize that no person or situation is wholly good or wholly bad and begin to appreciate it.
9. Do not be impatient at reasonable delays. One should have learned that he is not the arbiter of the universe and must often adjust oneself to other people at their convenience.
10. To endure defeat and disappointment without whining or complaining.
11. Do not worry about things one cannot help.
12. Not to boast or "show off" in socially unacceptable ways.
13. One should be honestly glad when others enjoy success or good fortune. One should outgrow envy and jealousy.
14. One should be open-minded enough to listen thoughtfully to the opinions of others.
15. One should plan things rather than trusting the inspiration of the moment.

In the opinion of Murray (2004), a mental hygiene person has the following characteristics, which are given in the box below:

CHARACTERISTICS OF MENTAL HYGIENE

1. The ability to give and receive alone.
2. The ability to face reality and deal with it.
3. Just as interested in giving as receiving.
4. The capacity to relate positively to life experiences.
5. The ability to learn from more experience.
6. The ability to accept frustration.
7. The ability to handle hostility constructively.
8. Relative freedom from tension symptoms.

SUGGESTIONS FOR DEVELOPING MENTAL HYGIENE

The following suggestions have been put forward through which mental hygiene can be improved.

1. **Love and sympathy:** These two traits are very important in the life of a person. Parents and teachers should try to develop these qualities among children. They should also love their children and deal with them sympathetically.

2. **Acceptance and recognition**: Lack of love and sympathy creates obstacles in the full development of the personality of the child. Hence, it is important that such an environment be created where the child has the feeling of self-acceptance and self-recognition. The parents and teachers should accept the child, despite his limitations, and provide due recognition where it is needed.
3. **Presenting as a role model**: The Teacher should be a role model and mentor for the child. He should set a good example for the students in the classroom.
4. **Games and cultural program**: In the school, there should be provision for sports and physical activities, so that the child may utilize his surplus energies in physical exercises. Similarly, the students should also be engaged in a cultural program. Provision should be made for the arrangement of co-curricular activities like debates, declamation contests, dramatics, and hobby classes, like painting, dancing, and music, etc., so that the students remain busy in these activities and develop their talents. In this way, they can be saved from the strains and stresses of life.
5. **Moral and religious training**: Moral and religious training should be given to children, because such a type of training can help in improving their mental health.
6. **Developing democratic values**: Ours is a democratic society. The school environment should also be democratic, where more emphasis should be given to developing mental health among students. This can be possible by imbibing democratic values among them.

CONCLUSION

Mental health is related to mental hygiene. Mental hygiene aims at the maintenance of mental health. In the twenty-first century, mental hygiene has changed its direction from that of cure to that of preservation, i.e., prevention of mental diseases and preservation of mental health. It is an age of stress, anxiety, depression, tension, conflict, frustration, and maladjustment. These give birth to many psychological problems that affect our mental health.

Mental health and mental hygiene can be seen as a continuum. Good mental health is generally viewed as a positive attribute. On the other hand, bad mental health is a sign of some kind of mental illness and a negative attribute. Here, the mental hygiene program plays a significant role in maintaining mental health. The definition of mental health also highlights emotional well-being, which imbibes the capacity to live a full and creative life, and the flexibility to deal with life's inevitable challenges.

Mental health and mental hygiene are closely related to life adjustment, emotional maturity, and a positive attitude towards the social environment. Life is an adjustment, whereas maladjustment leads to many mental disorders. Emotional maturity is a part of mental health and wellness. Emotional maturity is a behavioural state of mind with balanced feelings and self-control. A person who is emotionally stable and mature will have better adjustment with himself as well as with others. The emotional health of an individual depends on how his emotions have been developed.

3

PSYCHOLOGICAL WELL-BEING: NEED OF THE HOUR

INTRODUCTION

The concept of psychological well-being has attracted more attention from psychologists and behavioural scientists in the twenty-first century. The term psychological well-being has become very popular these days, as the quality of life, satisfaction with life, and happiness have been emphasized. It is also related to the mental health of a person, and hence, psychological well-being has acquired more importance. It also has a strong relationship with the emotional and social health of an individual. When psychological well-being is a well-talked-out issue, it becomes imperative to discuss its nature, concept, and its importance in daily life. After going through this chapter, the readers will be able to comprehend the following:

1. Nature and concept of psychological well-being
2. Different dimensions of psychological well-being
3. Factors of psychological well-being

CONCEPT OF PSYCHOLOGICAL WELL-BEING

Psychological well-being is concerned with subjective wellness, which is a measure of an individual's perceived level of life satisfaction and happiness. Psychological well-being is also related to self-concept, which may be stated as the totality of perceptions that each person has of himself. What a man thinks of himself and what he is. He knows his strengths and weaknesses. It also consists of his personality characteristics, including his level of self-confidence. His self-identity plays an important role in his psychological functioning.

Now, psychologists have started research work in positive psychology, which has emerged as a new area of psychology and is also a young branch of human behaviour. They are giving more attention to the concept of happiness, contentment, or life satisfaction. All these terms are related to psychological well-being. It is assumed that if one person is content, then his life goes well, and he is happy.

Psychological well-being or general well-being may be stated as the subjective feeling of contentment, happiness, satisfaction with life's experiences and role in the world of work, sense of achievement, and belonging, as well as no distress, grief, fear, dissatisfaction, or worry, etc. in his personal and social life. These things are difficult to assess objectively, hence the emphasis on the term 'subjective' well-being. It is related to but not dependent upon the physical/physiological conditions of a person, but it affects the mental and emotional health of human beings.

Psychological well-being may be defined as the total state of mental functioning of an individual who is well adjusted to his environment. The person experiences general feelings of enjoyment, job satisfaction, and a sense of identification with their role in the professional setting. Hence, the emphasis has been laid on the term 'subjective' or general well-being. Psychological well-being is not limited to physical, social, economic, or spiritual well-being, but rather encompasses total well-being, which includes both psychological and emotional wellness.

A new definition of psychological well-being is provided by Diener, Suh, Lucas, and Smith (1999), i.e., "Subjective well-being is a broad category of phenomena that includes people's emotional responses, domain satisfaction, and global judgments of life satisfaction." In general, psychological well-being is also known as human wellness. The concept of wellness is a dimension of attitude, behaviour, thoughts, and feelings, which can enhance a subjective sense of well-being and influence the individuals' attention to self-care and compliance with medical regimens.

Psychological well-being consists of emotional well-being and emotional intelligence, which is a new concept in the field of psychology. Both have very deep and strong relationships. Emotional intelligence leads to psychological well-being, whereas the latter helps to develop EIQ among human beings. So, it can be said that psychological well-being depends on emotional health and emotional intelligence. If a person has a higher level of emotional intelligence, he will have good emotional health and be an emotionally well-being person. Emotional intelligence refers to the ability to perceive, identify, manage, and assess emotions. The good news is that emotional intelligence can be acquired, learned, developed, and strengthened, as it is not an inborn characteristic.

The concept of psychological well-being has emerged from the connotation of mental ill health at the end of the 20th century. Now psychologists have started paying more attention in this 21st century, as they have accepted the two-factor theory of mental health, i.e., prevention and preservation, viz. the absence of psychological ill health. Many attempts have been made in the past to measure mental health, of which only one measures the subjective sense of psychological well-being.

Individual differences are found in the measures of psychological well-being in general because they incorporate a holistic approach emphasizing multiple dimensions that affect the quality of life, ultimately leading to a balanced, coordinated, healthy, and happy life. Psychological well-being includes personal, mental, emotional, and social well-being. Emotional well-being means to know, identify, understand, and express a full range of emotions and to channelize our emotions into healthy and constructive behaviours that help us to achieve our personal and social goals, whereas social well-being refers to whether an individual is well-adjusted in his environment and can get along well with others.

Psychological well-being leads to desirable consequences. It is often observed that what a society measures will, in turn, influence the things that it seeks. If a society takes great effort to measure productivity, people in society are likely to focus more on it, and sometimes even to the detriment of other values. If society regularly assesses its well-being, people will pay attention to it and learn more about its causes. Psychological well-being is, therefore, a valuable tool because it assesses well-being more directly, but it also has beneficial consequences.

NATURE OF WELL-BEING

Well-being is often used in the subject of philosophy, which describes what is ultimately good for a person. The question of what well-being consists of is of great importance in moral philosophy, according to which well-being is to be maximized. According to this view, known as welfarism, well-being is the only value system. In ethics, the question is how a person's moral character relates to his well-being. Well-being means how well a person's life is going for that person. A person's well-being is what is 'good for' him. Health, both physical and mental, might be said to be an important component of his well-being.

Well-being is a kind of value, sometimes called 'prudential value', to be distinguished from, for example, aesthetic value or moral value. For example, my giving money to a charity may have moral value, i.e., be morally good. And the effects of my donation may be good for others. But it remains an open question whether my being morally good is good for me; and, if it is, its being good for me is still conceptually distinct from its being morally good.

The philosophical use of the term consists of both positive and negative aspects of a person's life. The term, such as 'wellness', which covers how a person is behaving as a totality, whether good or bad, or 'happy' or sad, can be understood to balance between good and bad things in a person's life. So, philosophers use such terms in the more standard 'positive' way. But on the other hand, the well-being of somebody also means who is, and will remain, in the most terrible pain or agony: then their well-being is negative, and such that his life is worse for him rather than no life at all. The 'negative' aspects of how a person's life goes for them.

Well-being is a broader concept that includes happiness. Happiness is often used in ordinary life to refer to a short-lived state of a person, frequently a feeling of contentment and enjoyment. Philosophically, its scope is more often wider, encompassing a whole life. And, it is possible to speak of the happiness of a person's life, or his happy life, even if that person was usually miserable. The point is that some good things in their life have made it a happy one, even though they lacked contentment. So, well-being is related to the total functioning of the mental processes of a person.

According to Layard (2006), "Since happiness is subjective and it is difficult to assess, it has been shown that happiness does not necessarily increase correspondingly with the comfort that results from increasing income. As a result, the standard of living should not be taken to be a measure of happiness". During the last few decades, psychologists have paid more attention to the notion of 'happiness'. Such happiness is usually understood in terms of contentment or 'life-satisfaction'. When debating the idea of what makes life good for the individual living that life, it is preferable to use the term 'well-being' instead of 'happiness'.

TYPES OF WELL-BEING

While well-being means a healthy, wealthy, and prosperous life, the meaning of well-being also includes:

- Well-being gives the maximum energy for the sake of enjoyment in life.
- It gives a feeling of happiness and contentment in our daily life.
- It helps to develop skills, knowledge, and a positive attitude.
- It includes having affectionate and cordial relationships.
- It leads to vulnerability to illness.
- It produces commitment, control, and challenge to be the best person in life.

Well-being is achieved only when you are healthy in all areas. Your body, mind, and soul are in a state of balance, and you are a whole person. Total health is complete health from all angles, which includes physical, mental, emotional, and social wellness. To define well-being, we need to include all aspects of well-being and health. Total well-being includes the following types, which are shown in the following box:

TYPES OF WELL-BEING
1. Intellectual well-being 2. Emotional well-being 3. Social well-being 4. Spiritual well-being 5. Physical well-being

All these types have been described below:

1. **Intellectual well-being:** Well-being includes many cognitive abilities, like perception, intelligence, and aptitude, that affect our lifestyle. Problem-solving skills and good decision-making abilities mean ensuring that a healthy mental attitude is maintained. All these powers are included in intellectual well-being. Well-being includes self-awareness, positive thoughts, and right mental functioning, which may affect one's lifestyle.
2. **Emotional well-being:** Another important part of total well-being is emotional well-being. Emotional well-being means the awareness of our emotions and the ability to maintain and control our aroused feelings. The ability to shift a negative emotion to a positive one and to resolve conflicts realistically is a characteristic of emotional well-being. To change negative emotions to positive ones by using problem-solving techniques to resolve conflicts. Emotional well-being means an awareness of one's feelings, emotions, and attitudes, as well as the ability to maintain emotional maturity.
3. **Social well-being**: Social well-being consists of social adjustment and maturity. A social group helps to support a wellness lifestyle. Empathy and active listening skills are important for nurturing friendships and offer a state of happiness to support social well-being. It ensures a supportive social environment, which helps a healthy and wealthy lifestyle. If anybody is actively applying some social skills in the company of other people who are enjoying friendships, then they will be in a state of happiness and ecstasy to maintain social well-being.
4. **Spiritual well-being:** Spiritual well-being means a sense of religious values and spirituality, and connection with healthy moral values for better living. Understanding personal values and purpose, if a person has a feeling of spirituality and has imbibed healthy moral values and the righteous purpose of life, he will have spiritual well-being.

5. **Physical well-being:** Physical well-being is related to the physical health of an individual. It is one part of total well-being. Physical fitness is the basic requirement for total health as well as the total well-being of a person. We should stay focused on taking care of our bodies with proper nutrition, exercise, adequate sleep, and avoiding wrong habits such as alcohol, drugs, tobacco, etc. We should find time for regular physical exercise and relaxation to help the body and mind stay fit and healthy.

DIMENSIONS OF PSYCHOLOGICAL WELL-BEING

Psychological well-being consists of many dimensions, including emotional health, emotional well-being, mental well-being, life satisfaction, and quality of life. These dimensions are being discussed below:

1. **Emotional health:** Emotional health, which is a part of mental health, is very much related to psychological well-being. Emotional health has many aspects, e.g., emotional well-being, adjustment in life, and emotional maturity. The mental components needed to handle emotional problems will give us a base for mental and emotional health. Basically, emotional health depends on self-esteem, i.e., how we perceive ourselves and the behaviour that is appropriate and healthy.

   Every person may suffer from some minor psychological problems. But emotionally healthy people can easily adjust to and solve their problems. They also help others to get life satisfaction and enjoy themselves with others.

2. **Emotional well-being:** Emotional well-being is one of the most important dimensions of psychological well-being and mental health. Now, this concept has acquired more importance these days. It is much more related to emotional health. Emotional well-being is a measure of an individual's perceived level of happiness and life satisfaction. There is a relationship between self-concept and emotional well-being as well as emotional intelligence. An emotionally intelligent person can solve problems and manage stress. He has more impulse control and a positive attitude.

   Emotional well-being may have the characteristics of contentment, enjoyment, self-sufficiency, and self-assurance in life, resiliency, and the ability to cope with life's ups and downs, and a sense of honesty of purpose in life. He can easily manage strains and stresses, as well as storms and struggles. The capacity to develop cordial and satisfying relationships with other people is the main quality of emotional well-being. It is also related to the spiritual and social dimensions of life or the social adjustments of individuals. Knowing our strengths and weaknesses, controlling anger effectively, solving internal conflict, and communicating efficiently and meaningfully with others all play important roles in a positive state of emotional wellness.

Emotional well-being is the behavioural aspect of an individual to think well and to feel good in an objective and constructive way. It is the mental functioning of a person that determines how he feels and thinks about himself and those others surrounding him. Many people equate emotional well-being with happiness. Many people think that to achieve emotional well-being, all must be well in one's life. People tend to associate emotional well-being with positive emotions.

3. **Mental well-being**: Psychological well-being is also related to mental well-being, which is a part of mental health. Mental wellness is generally seen as a positive attribute when a person reaches the top level of mental health. This sign of mental health highlights mental well-being, i.e., the capacity to live a full and creative life, and the adaptability to deal with life's inevitable challenges and difficulties. Many therapeutic measures are effective for improving the mental well-being of normal and healthy people.

   To know about mental well-being, it is necessary to understand the concepts of mental health, emotional health, and social adjustment. Mental well-being is related to personal satisfaction and social acceptance, and it is that condition which makes it possible for the individual to meet lifelong problems in such ways as providing him with a feeling of self-satisfaction and to contribute optimally to the satisfaction and welfare of the social group.

   The chracteristics of a mentally well-being person are:

   (i) He should be able to relax both the mind and body.
   (ii) There should be the absence of stress, anxiety, and tension.
   (iii) He should possess a sense of psychological security.
   (iv) He should have a feeling of self-worth and self-satisfaction.
   (v) He should have the ability to deal effectively with the reality of life.
   (vi) He should feel enjoyment in human relationships.
   (vii) He should possess the capability to enjoy mutual satisfaction in social relationships.
   (viii) He should be able to integrate socially useful activities.
   (ix) He should have the quality of dynamism and flexibility.
   (x) He should be able to maintain a balance between self-efficacy and will to help others.

(xi) He should have the capacity to give and get affection.

(xii) He possesses the ability to convert hostile feelings into constructive ways.

(xiii) He can modify the present frustration into a future gain.

(xiv) He is willing to enjoy life spontaneously.

(xv) He can learn from past failures.

Some of the above-mentioned characteristics enable an individual to meet adequately the demands of the social situation. Considering mental well-being in a social context, it may be said that mental well-being is expressed in social adjustment. An example of a mental wellness model includes one developed by Myers, Sweeney, and Witmer (1990). It includes five life tasks—(i) essence or spirituality, (ii) work and leisure, (iii) friendship, (iv) love and (v) self-direction—and twelve sub-tasks—sense of worth, sense of control, realistic beliefs, emotional awareness and coping, problem solving and creativity, sense of humor, nutrition, exercise, self-care, stress management, gender identity, and cultural identity—which are identified as characteristics of healthy functioning and a major component of wellness. Components provide a means of responding to the circumstances of life in a manner that promotes healthy functioning.

4. **Life satisfaction and well-being:** Life satisfaction is another aspect of psychological well-being, which is used to assess happiness in life. It is concerned with the lifestyle of an individual. It represents how satisfied people feel with their lives generally. Life satisfaction means how people think about their life, whether they are achieving their goals, doing well in their jobs, or having job satisfaction. Whether they get along well with other people around them. Life satisfaction is thus a more comprehensive term.

Life satisfaction is very much relevant; it is used in determining happiness in life. Life satisfaction and happiness are very much related to each other. It means that life satisfaction involves how people think about their contentment in life, their surroundings, as well as the fact that other people around them are also happy, contented, and satisfied. Happiness with the present state of life is an important predictor of life satisfaction. But happiness is sometimes used interchangeably with life satisfaction, quality of life, and psychological well-being. But life satisfaction is one of the important factors of wellness.

The signs of life satisfaction are given in the following box:

SIGNS OF LIFE SATISFACTION
1. One should be mentally ready to change one's life. 2. One can make peace with past experiences. 3. One should plan for future life. 4. One should be satisfied with others' viewpoints.

Life satisfaction is a complex concept as compared to the attainment of goals or feeling good about oneself. Life satisfaction is an objective evaluation of feelings and attitudes about one's life at a particular time, ranging from positive to negative. It is one of three major indicators of well-being: life satisfaction, positive effect, and negative effect (Diener, 1984).

5. **Quality of life and well-being:** Quality of life is an important concept in psychological well-being, but it is a broader concept than standard of living. However, the standard of living is usually measured in financial and economic conditions of the family, which cannot be compared with the quality of life experienced by some people.

The term *quality of life* is being used to assess the general well-being of individuals and societies. The term is used in various fields, e.g., inter-personal development, education, healthcare, and politics. On the other hand, the standard of living includes wealth, money, materialistic rewards, and good employment, as well as the physical and social environment. But the quality of life consists not only of wealth and employment, but also the total environment, including physical and mental health, education, recreation and leisure time, and social belonging (Gregory, et al. 2009).

Quality of life is an important aspect of emotional development. Many attempts have been made to improve the quality of life for individuals or groups. It is all concerned with the economic conditions of society. But the economic development of the country helps in the development of the psychological well-being of its citizens.

Quality of life is often considered within the field of medical health care, and how it affects the life of an individual from a physical and mental health point of view. On the other hand, the standard of living makes an objective or long-term assessment of the quality of life experienced by people in society. Psychological well-being has two main aspects, i.e., personal well-being and emotional well-being, when people are rated about their quality of daily emotional experiences, e.g., joy, stress, sadness, anger, and affection. People are also asked about their lives in general and are evaluated against a measure (Kahneman & Deaton, 2010). The quality of life is based on who one is, how one is connected to one's environment, and whether one achieves one's personal and social goals, hopes, and aspirations.

PSYCHOLOGICAL WELL-BEING AND SELF-CONCEPT

Psychological Well-being is very much related to self-concept. Self-concept refers to an individual's perception of "self." It is simply an individual's awareness of himself. Self-concept is a multidimensional personality construct that refers to an individual's perception of "oneself" in the context of several characteristics, e.g., family, gender roles, racial identity, job involvement, nationality, and many more. Self-concept is also called self-mirror, self-picture, or self-sufficiency, self-assurance, self-regard, and self-efficacy, etc.

The self-concept has cognitive, affective, and conative domains of behaviour, which means how people think, feel, and act, as well as how they try to assess themselves. The self-concept is a general term that refers to how someone may think or perceive oneself. Hence, the term self-concept may be used as the totality of perceptions that each person has of himself, and this self-image plays an important role in the psychological functioning of people.

Self-concept consists of four aspects: (i) how a person perceives himself, (ii) what he thinks of himself, (iii) how he values himself, and (iv) how he attempts through various actions to enhance his self-image. Guilford (1966) defined self-concept as "an individual's perception, attitude, and feeling about himself." There seemed to be positive and negative dimensions of self-concept. The characteristics of self-concept comprise personality traits, skills, attitudes, knowledge, and abilities, along with job requirements, hobbies, and physical traits, etc.

Moreover, self-concept is not only concerned with the present, but it also consists of the past and future. It is related to what has already gone. Now, planning for future life also consists of self-concept. In the future, what would you like to be, or what would you like to become, or what would you aim to achieve in your future life? These aspirations and ambitions may work as incentives for future planning.

The humanistic psychologists like Carl Rogers, Abraham Maslow, and many others who belonged to the Humanistic School of Psychology paved the way for this concept. According to Rogers (1961), everyone strives to become more like an "ideal self." There is always a discrepancy between the real self and the ideal self. The closer one is to their ideal self, the happier they will be. Rogers also gave the idea of *unconditional positive regard* (UPR), which is one factor in a person's happiness that often occurs in close or familial relationships and involves a consistent level of the ideal self.

Rogers (1961) says, "Self-concept includes all our thoughts, ideas, and judgments about ourselves. It shows how we perceive ourselves, whether good, bad, or neutral. Self-concept does not necessarily reflect reality; a person can be smart, warm, and successful but still have a negative self-concept, or have a positive self-concept even though he may be immoral or despised by others." A strong positive self-concept that is realistic and not too different from what we would ideally like to be is the goal of human beings, according to Rogers. The individual needs to receive positive regard from others as well as from the self. *Unconditional positive regard* (UPR) by others facilitates self-regard and makes our self-concept strong and positive. However, most of us grow up in such an environment where love is conditional.

According to Rogers, problems arise when people 's behaviours do not conform to their self-concepts. If there is a discrepancy between what you do and what you think you are, you will experience anxiety. The wider the gap between our actions and our self-image, the greater the anxiety and tension. The healthy reaction to this disparity between our behaviours and our self-concept is to acknowledge the behaviour and feelings, rather than deny them.

Carl Rogers believes that the self-concept has the following characteristics given in the box:

CHARACTERISTICS OF SELF-CONCEPT

1. The image you have of yourself (Self-image).
2. How much value do you place on yourself (self-esteem or self-worth).
3. What you wish you would look like (Ideal self).
4. Self-picture (what you see in yourself).

Guilford (1966) writes, "There has been a growing realization of the importance of self-concept in recent years in understanding and predicting human behaviour and well-being. Self-concept is how the individual reacts to himself for his perceptions, attitudes, and feelings. This is the totality of an individual's behaviour through which he manages difficult situations. Self-concept is not an inherited quality. It is formed because of one's experiences and reaction to the environment."

FACTORS OF PSYCHOLOGICAL WELL-BEING

Psychological well-being is a multifaceted concept. It is a subjective term that means different things to different people. It is related to contentment, life satisfaction, self-actualization, peace, and happiness. The characteristics of psychological well-being are the personality traits that a person can't achieve at the same time. A person with "psychological well-being" is a happy, go-lucky, and well-satisfied person. The factors that contribute to a person's psychological well-being have been shown in the following box.

FACTORS AFFECTING PSYCHOLOGICAL WELL-BEING

1. Sense of achievement or feeling of accomplishment.
2. Feeling of utilizing one's full abilities.
3. Acceptance of work by officers or recognition of work by superiors.
4. Appreciation of work by colleagues or peers.
5. Promotion in status and pay & salary.

The factors which affect psychological well-being are described below:

1. **Sense of achievement:** The main factor that affects the psychological well-being of a person is the feeling of accomplishment. He feels that his work is appreciated by others. The level of achievement and his performance are closer to his expectations, then he will be very satisfied. This factor is related to the need for achievement or achievement motivation, which is an important factor for psychological well-being. Even for the development of personality, a person needs achievement.
2. **Feeling of utilizing one's abilities:** Every man is born with some potential which develops some abilities, capacities, and capabilities to be used in life. If he gets the opportunity to utilize his potential to the maximum limit, he will be successful, and his psychological well-being will be at the top. These competencies must be developed to their maximum level, so that people may develop based on their potential.
3. **Recognition of the work by superiors:** Every worker wants his officers to recognize his work, and he gets appreciation from them. Recognition, achievement, and mental security are the secondary needs that are essential for the development of one's personality. If a worker perceives that his work is being accepted and applauded by his seniors and gets some rewards in terms of recognition or materialistic incentives, he will be very happy not only intrinsically, but also extrinsically. This is a sign of psychological well-being.
4. **Appreciation of the work by colleagues and peers:** If a person finds that his friends, peers, co-workers, and colleagues approve of the accomplishments which he has achieved, he will be more than satisfied. If all other people appreciate the work done by

him and are happy with his performance, he will be satisfied and contented. Psychological well-being depends upon the feeling that one's work is socially recognized.

5. **Promotion in status and pay and salary:** Another important factor of psychological well-being is that every worker must get a promotion in his professional career. Every good worker must be promoted to his status after a minimum period of five to eight years. If he gets two or three increments in his professional life, his psychological well-being will also be very high. It is related to the need for status and power. It is very important for the growth and development of an individual.

The implication is that we all need a purpose in our lives to be "happy". The worker needs to feel that s/he has a purpose and has a need that can be fulfilled.

RYFF'S MODEL OF PSYCHOLOGICAL WELL-BEING

Psychological well-being is often considered one of the hallmarks of mental health and emotional well-being. Carol Ryff (1995) has done much research work in psychological well-being and constructed and standardized a scale for measuring psychological well-being. According to her," Well-being is a dynamic concept that includes subjective, social, and psychological dimensions as well as health-related behaviours." This test specifically focuses on measuring multiple facets of psychological well-being, which are given in the box below:

MULTIPLE FACETS OF PSYCHOLOGICAL WELL-BEING

1. Self-acceptance
2. Positive relations with others
3. Autonomy
4. Environmental mastery
5. Purpose in life
6. Personal growth

All the above-mentioned facets of psychological well-being fall to a continuum, from very high to very low. Their description is given below:

1. **Self-acceptance**: According to Ryff, self-acceptance is the main factor of psychological well-being. A person with a high level of self-acceptance has a positive attitude toward life and accepts many aspects of the self, which include both good and bad qualities. He has no regrets about his past life. On the other hand, a person

with low self-acceptance is not satisfied with himself and has a negative attitude towards life. Usually, he is frustrated with what he has attained in life, regrets his past experiences, and feels pain and anger regarding something that has happened. Moreover, he wants to be a different person than he is at present.

2. **Positive relations with others:** A person with *positive relations with other people has* strong bonds with others. He has a warm, satisfying, cordial, and affectionate relationship with others. Moreover, he is interested in the well-being of others, capable of having strong feelings of empathy, love, and intimacy, and has feelings of giving and taking in human relationships. On the other hand, a man with negative relations with others *will have a negative attitude in life* and will not be warm, open, and concerned about others. He remains aloof and alone in interpersonal relationships. He is not willing to maintain important ties with others.

3. **Autonomy**: The person with high *psychological well-being will have a sense of autonomy in thought and action. Autonomy* is a self-determining and independent way of thinking. He has his own viewpoint in life and may differ with others, though he can tolerate social pressures to think and act in certain ways. He is free to do whatever he wants to do, but within the limits of social taboos and societal norms. He can manage his behaviour and evaluate himself by personal standards. On the other hand, a person with low autonomy *is* concerned about the expectations and evaluations of others' standards and relies on judgments of others to make important decisions; conform to social pressures to think and act in certain ways.

4. **Environmental mastery**: The person with *high environmental mastery can* handle complex environments that suit his personal needs and motives. He has a sense of mastery and competence in managing the environment and controls the complexities of external activities. *On the other hand, a person with low environmental mastery has* difficulty in managing daily routine-type activities. He is unable to improve the surrounding environment, is not aware of coming opportunities, and lacks a sense of control over the external world.

5. **Purpose in life:** A person with high *purpose in life has* the pursuit of excellence in the past, present, and future lives. He holds beliefs that give purpose to life and has high aims for living. *On the other hand, a person with a low purpose in life lacks* a sense of meaning and honesty of purpose in life. He has not set any goals or has set very few goals. He lacks a sense of direction for his future life and does not see anything in his past life. He has no outlook or belief that may give any meaning to his present life.

6. **Personal growth:** A person with *high personal growth has* a feeling of continued growth and development. He sees himself as growing and developing. He is open to new experiences; has a sense of achieving his potential, sees improvement in life and behaviour. On *the other hand, a person with low personal growth* has a sense of personal stagnation; lacks a sense of improvement or development over time. He feels dejected and uninterested in life. He is unable to develop positive attitudes or positive thinking.

   The concept of psychological well-being has faced some challenges and controversies. In the recent past, well-being had little effect on some people. Because the construct of psychological well-being in the past was non-existent, non-theoretical concepts were used. Nowadays, the concept of psychological well-being is being used frequently.

CONCLUSION

Psychological well-being refers to the overall condition of the mental health and emotional well-being of an individual. It includes the way we feel about ourselves, the quality of our relationships, and our ability to manage our feelings and face the difficulties and problems bravely. Being mentally or emotionally well-being means that a person is free from stress, anxiety, depression, or other psychological problems. It also refers to the presence of positive traits of personality. Psychological well-being consists of many dimensions, including emotional health, emotional well-being, mental well-being, life satisfaction, and quality of life.

Psychological well-being means the longevity of life, with the absence of any kind of physical or mental illness or abnormalities. The more we live healthily, the more happiness we derive from our healthy life. It includes the way we feel about ourselves, the quality of our relationships, and our ability to manage our feelings and deal with difficulties. Psychological well-being includes subjective well-being, quality of life, satisfaction in life, happiness, and mental health. It is also related to self-concept and self-esteem. There are many factors that affect the psychological well-being of an individual. Ryff has given her own multifaceted model of psychological well-being.

4

MENTAL HEALTH AND HUMAN WELLNESS

INTRODUCTION

Human wellness is related to the mental health of human beings. Human wellness is concerned with the behavioural skills that are associated with human well-being. It aims to make life more comfortable as well as to help people be happier and healthier. So, the concept of human wellness has acquired more importance in this current era, when most people are victims of strain and stress. Now, more emphasis is being given to the mental health and emotional well-being of the people. So, the concept of human wellness has become more popular. The synonymous words being used are psychological well-being, subjective wellness, general well-being, quality of life, satisfaction, happiness, and lifestyle.

Quality of life and life satisfaction are components of an individual's perceived level of human wellness. Human wellness is closely related to the psychological well-being of an individual. Of course, the latter is concerned with the mental and emotional health of a man. Psychological well-being may be stated as the general feelings of enjoyment, happiness, contentment, job satisfaction at the workplace, a sense of achievement, and belonging, as well as the absence of distress, dissatisfaction, fear, or worry, etc.

CONCEPT OF HUMAN WELLNESS

The concept of wellness has attracted attention from psychologists and behavioural scientists in the present day of turmoil, when people are suffering from strains and stresses. It is very much related to mental health. Now, psychologists have started working on subjects like 'quality of life, happiness, enjoyment, and mental satisfaction', and hence, the term human wellness has become very popular.

Human wellness may be defined as "the global state of mental functioning of an individual who wants to be well-adjusted to both physical and social environments. Usually, a child is born with a clean slate with no ill will, grief, anger, or" any other remorse. He is a happy-go-lucky child, but when he grows up, due to various types of environmental influences and stimuli that affect his daily life, he becomes either a notorious man or a pious person. But he wants to lead a normal human life. He may seek to have general feelings of enjoyment, contentment, and happiness, satisfaction with one's experiences, and job satisfaction in the professional life. Moreover, he does not want to experience grief, fear, or worry, etc., in his personal and social life. Hence, the emphasis has been laid on the term 'subjective' or general well-being. Human wellness is not confined to physical, social, economic, or spiritual well-being, but it is a total well-being. It also includes psychological and emotional wellness.

In general terms, psychological well-being is also known as wellness. The concept of human wellness is a dimension of attitude, behaviour, thoughts, and feelings, which can enhance a general sense of well-being, and which affects the individual's attention to self-care and medical care. Human wellness is a multifaceted domain of psychological well-being.

The concept of human wellness consists of the mental health and emotional well-being of an individual, as well as the moral and ethical values of a person. Life is complex, and so people encounter failures, defeats, frustrations, and disappointments in their lives. But it is the mental mechanism of the person that helps to cope with their failures, frustrations, and negative aspects of their life. In this way, they have the strength and wisdom to move forward and come out of the darkness of life. They can achieve a state of wellness or well-being. So, it is the balance of the person's mind that brings a peaceful state amid the difficulties of life and helps them to achieve their goals in life.

For a common man, wellness is related to economic gains, but it is also related to mental satisfaction and a peaceful state of mind. People often place more emphasis on materialistic materials rather than internal beauty and the virtues of life. If society starts giving importance to internal qualities, then people will understand the value of wellness. Human wellness has many ramifications for an individual, as well as helping him to create a peaceful and stable society.

There is a positive relationship between human wellness and emotional well-being. The term human wellness has a different connotation for every individual, but it has a big effect on the quality of life, leading to a balanced, healthy, and happy life. Human wellness includes mental, emotional, and social well-being. Emotional well-being helps us to identify, recognize, understand, and manage emotions for our benefit as well as for others' benefit, and to channelize our emotions into socially acceptable behaviour patterns and a healthy way of life that satisfies our personal and social needs. On the other hand, social well-being means that an individual is well-adjusted in his environment.

Human wellness or emotional well-being depends on emotional intelligence. If a person has a higher emotional quotient (EQ) he will have good emotional health, and he will be an emotionally well-being person. EIQ reveals how a human person identifies, understands, and controls his own emotions and intense feelings. It refers to the ability to perceive, recognize, manage, and evaluate emotions for our welfare and others' welfare.

Besides emotional intelligence, the concept of human wellness is also related to emotional maturity, social adjustment, and mental toughness. It may also have a positive and high correlation with quality of life, job satisfaction/general life satisfaction, sense of achievement, etc. On the other hand, human wellness has a negative relationship with some minor or major mental disorders, like stress, anxiety, phobias, depression, paranoia, schizophrenia, etc.

The contention about mental disorders or mental health problems seems to have been replaced by human wellness in the last decade of the 20th century. We may expect greater attention for human wellness at the beginning of the 21st century, accepting the two-factor theory of mental health: (i) prevention of mental disorders, and (ii) preservation of mental health. Many attempts have been made in the past to measure positive mental health, which is the measure of a subjective and general sense of human wellness.

In recent years, many research studies have been conducted on human wellness (Diener & Diener, 1995). Human wellness has been considered in the context of the experience of an individual (Campbell et al. 1976), which is his/her responses to his or her life, whether in terms of life satisfaction or positive emotional reactions. Diener & Diener (1995), however, contended that no attention was paid to whether the characteristics of human wellness differ in various cultures.

MEANING OF WELLNESS

According to the Dictionary meaning, the word "well" means: (i) good or sound in body and mind, (ii) proper, fitting, or gratifying. The word "ness" means: (i) the fact of existing; (ii) conscious, or existence of life. Combining these two words, wellness is the state of consciously experiencing the existence of our feelings, like joy, sorrow, fear, hate, and love, at any given time. It is related to our emotional behaviour. So, human wellness means managing your emotions objectively and consciously. Human wellness consists of emotional well-being or emotional wellness. People tend to associate emotional wellness with positive emotions or emotions that make you feel happy and good.

Wellness is a broader concept that includes happiness. Wellness is related to the overall state of mind of a person. Wellness is the notion of how well a person's life is going. A person's wellness is what is good for himself. Health, then, might be said to be a constituent of his wellness. Wellness is also one of two aspects of personal well-being, the other being 'life evaluation'. This topic is of great interest to psychologists and other health professionals.

A definition of wellness includes living in a state of optimal well-being, i.e., the opposite of living with chronic stress. Living a lifestyle that nurtures wellness helps prevent mental disorders, which may cause distress or negative stress. Managing stress requires a conscious effort to maintain a balanced lifestyle of relaxation, using good coping strategies, gaining skills for effective communication, and altering behaviours to have a happier and healthier life. Good physical and mental health leads to wellness, i.e., the absence of any stress or anxiety in life, and changing attitudes to have a prosperous life.

Having a lifestyle that nurtures well-being helps to prevent grief and distress, or negative thoughts. A balanced and effective lifestyle teaches one how to manage stress, reduce tension, control anxiety, and resolve conflict, which requires a conscious effort on the part of an individual. He makes use of relaxation exercises, applies good coping strategies to learn some psychological skills, and uses effective communication to have a happier and healthier life. The key points of the concept of wellness have been highlighted in the following box:

CONCEPT OF WELLNESS
1. To have maximum vigor and energy to enjoy life. 2. To have a feeling of satisfaction, contentment, and happiness. 3. To increase self-knowledge and develop abilities. 4. To have cordial, loving, and satisfactory relationships. 5. To have low vulnerability towards illness. 6. To have commitment, control, and challenge in your life.

DIMENSIONS OF WELLNESS

Like psychological well-being, human wellness also consists of eight mutually interdependent dimensions, e.g., physical, intellectual, emotional, social, spiritual, vocational, financial, and environmental, which are given in the following Table:

TABLE: DIMENSIONS OF WELLNESS

1. **Physical Dimension:** We should care for our bodies to stay healthy now as well as in the future.
2. **Intellectual Dimension:** We should develop intellectually based on our potential, and we should be curious to learn and respond positively to intellectual challenges. We should expand our knowledge and skills to work productively in our lives.
3. **Emotional Dimension:** We should try to understand our feelings, values, and attitudes as well as appreciate the feelings of others. We should manage our emotions and feelings positively and constructively.
4. **Social Dimension:** We should maintain healthy relationships, and try to enjoy ourselves with others, develop friendships and intimate relations, care about others, and let others care about you.
5. **Spiritual Dimension:** We should find purpose, value, and meaning in our lives with or without participating in activities that are consistent with our beliefs and values.
6. **Vocational Dimension:** We should prepare ourselves and participate in work that provides personal satisfaction and life enrichment that is consistent with our values, goals, and lifestyle.
7. **Financial Dimension:** We should try to manage our resources to live within our means, setting realistic goals, and preparing for short-term and long-term emergencies. We should be aware that everyone's financial values, needs, and circumstances are unique.
8. **Environmental Dimension:** We should understand how our social, natural, and physical environments affect our health and well-being.

Human wellness is a general term that has different connotations for different people. It is like self-realization, which is a feeling of accomplishment in life and brings peace and happiness. A person with "wellness" is a happy and satisfied person.

FACTORS OF HUMAN WELLNESS

The factors that affect a person's wellness include the following:

1. Achievement Motivation
2. Use of One's Potential
3. Social Acceptance
4. Recognition by Friends and Peers
5. Promotional Avenues
6. Need for Status and Power

1. **Achievement Motivation:** Achievement motivation or the need for achievement, is one of the important factors of human wellness. It is one variable of human motivation. It is one of the secondary needs of a person. If this need is not satisfied, that person will develop a personality malfunction. So, for the development of personality, an individual should have feelings of achievement, motivation, or a need for achievement.
2. **Use of One's Potential:** Every man is born with some potential, though he inherits it from the genes of his parent. From potential, he develops abilities, intelligence, capacities, and capabilities. He wants to utilize his abilities to its full use. For human wellness, these competencies must be developed to their maximum level. Whatever level of abilities is found, they must be utilized. If they remain unutilized, this may cause havoc and create crises in a man.
3. **Social Acceptance:** Every person feels that he should be accepted by other people in society. He should get love and affection from others. Whatever he does, he should be appreciated and rewarded for his good work. If an individual is not socially accepted, he would feel an inferiority complex and may develop some personality problems.
4. **Recognition by Friends and Peers:** It is also an important factor in human wellness. Every child and even an elderly person wants their action to be applauded by others. He should be recognized in his group, as he is an important member. In this way, he fulfills his need for affiliation or a feeling of belonging.
5. **Promotion Avenues:** It is very important for the growth of an individual. Every person wants to grow professionally. Whether a person is in a private or government job, or working at his own business, or in some other profession, he should get an opportunity to show his worth, talent, and skill. Due to his hard work at his job, he must get his due promotion, which will be a good incentive to put more effort and hard work into his professional duties. So, every employee must get opportunities for promotion.
6. **Need for Status and Power:** This factor of human wellness is concerned with salary and wages. An individual must get sufficient salary and wages for doing any professional work, so that he may lead a happy and prosperous life. It is related to the need for status and power.

Many other factors contribute to a person's wellness. The implication is that we all need a goal in our lives to be "happy". According to Carol Ryff (1995)," Wellness is a dynamic concept that includes personal, social, and psychological dimensions as well as health-related problems." It focuses specifically on measuring multiple dimensions of human wellness.

MENTAL HEALTH AND HUMAN WELLNESS

Mental health and human wellness are well-connected with each other. Sometimes, mental health is equated with the wellness of a human being. Wellness is the process of practicing a daily healthy lifestyle to achieve better physical and mental health results. To know the importance of wellness, it's essential to understand its relationship with mental health. Wellness is commonly considered to have seven different dimensions, which may include mental, physical, social, financial, spiritual, environmental, and vocational. These dimensions are interdependent and affect each other.

Wellness is an active process of being aware of and selecting something towards a healthy lifestyle. It is a dynamic process of change and growth, i.e., a satisfactory living condition, a state of mental health, happiness, prosperity, and psychological well-being. It is not only the absence of any mental disorder, like anxiety, depression, obsession, compulsion, or phobias. "Health is a state of complete physical, mental, and social well-being (World Health Organization, 2005). It has been defined as "an integrated life functioning, which is directed toward maximizing the potential of the individual." It is the quality of life that promotes wellness.

Wellness is an approach to healthcare that emphasizes preventing illness and prolonging life, as compared to cure and treatment. Wellness means the state of good physical, mental, emotional, and social health. It means that a good life is maintained by an appropriate diet, exercise, and other lifestyle changes. It is the state of being healthy, wealthy, and prosperous that you are actively trying to achieve. Yoga and shavasana are said to promote the wellness of the mind and body.

Wellness is the conscious and unconscious development of the whole self. To achieve wellness, firstly, the appropriate tools must be selected to make you a healthier and happier human being. Then these tools are to be used for continued growth and development. There are countless methods to cultivate yourself on an ever-changing path of wellness.

The Global Wellness Institute defines wellness *as the active pursuit of activities, choices, and lifestyles that lead to a state of holistic health, which includes* mental health. There are two important aspects of this viewpoint. First, wellness is not a passive or static state but rather an "active pursuit" that is associated with holistic health, i.e., it goes beyond physical health and incorporates many different dimensions. It consists of an active process of being aware and making choices that lead toward an outcome of optimal holistic health and well-being.

MODEL OF HUMAN WELLNESS

Wellness is Multidimensional: One model of wellness includes at least six dimensions. This model was devised by Dr. Jack Travis (Illness-Wellness Continuum).

The above dimensions are described below:

1. **Physical:** One should keep oneself physically fit and nourish a healthy body through exercise, nutrition, sleep, etc.
2. **Mental:** One should be mentally alert by engaging himself through learning, problem-solving, decision-making, and creativity, etc.
3. **Emotional:** One should be emotionally mature by being aware of and expressing our feelings and understanding the feelings of others.
4. **Spiritual:** One should be spiritually high by searching for a meaningful and higher purpose in human life.
5. **Social:** One should be socially adjusted by connecting with others and communities in meaningful ways.
6. **Environmental:** One should be satisfied with the environment by fostering positive relationships between healthy human actions and well-being.

According to the author of this model, one way to understand wellness is to consider health as a continuum that extends from illness to a state of optimal well-being. On one hand, patients with poor health engage medical programs to treat illnesses. On the other hand, people focus proactively on the prevention of mental illnesses. They develop attitudes and lifestyles that prevent disease, improve health, and enhance their quality of life and feelings of well-being.

MINDFULNESS IN HUMAN WELLNESS

Mindfulness is a new concept in human wellness. Mindfulness is the basic human ability to be aware of what we are, where we are, and what we are going to do. Mindfulness is a quality that every human being should possess. It is a mental state of the human being that is achieved by focusing one's awareness on the present situation. So, it is a state of being conscious or aware of something. Richards, Campania, and Muse-Burk (2010) found, "mindfulness is considered to be a purposeful state; it may be that those who practice it believe in its importance and value being mindful, so that valuing of self-care activities may influence the intentional component of mindfulness".

Mindfulness means that we should concentrate on our thoughts and feelings, without considering what is "right" or what is "wrong". We should not regret some adverse happenings and try to forget them. But we should accept what is in our present or what we have in our surroundings and not remorse what is not there now or what we could not achieve in the past. There is nothing good or bad but thinking makes it so. What matters is what we are getting now or what we are thinking now. It is a way of thinking or feeling in each situation. When we apply mindfulness, our thoughts concentrate on what we are feeling in the present situation rather than thinking about the future. Mindfulness is a way of being that helps us to feel more aware of the present. In a practical exercise, we should try to concentrate on any one point on our forehead and try to concentrate on our feelings.

Mindfulness is not innate, but an acquired or learned exercise that can be cultivated through some therapeutic methods, particularly through yoga and meditation. When we do meditation, it gives us some peace of mind as well as a calm and quiet state of mental functioning. When we are in a state of mindfulness, we manage stress, enhance performance, achieve accomplishment, get insight and awareness through introspection and observation, and increase our concentration in our mind for human wellness.

The exercise of mindfulness is very simple. You try to focus your attention on your present experience and concentrate on your feelings. Intrinsically, you try to introspect what is happening in your surroundings and what is going on around you in your environment. You try to notice any thoughts, emotions, or sensations that are occurring in different parts of your body. This may look simple, but you are likely to face some hurdles on the way. You may feel tension, restless, sleepy, and sometimes bored, or confused. This technique of mindfulness will enable you to overcome these obstacles. It is a learning process. Mindfulness helps us to be more aware of what is going on here and not be affected by our strong feelings, emotions, and thoughts, which may cause stress, anxiety, negative feelings, frustration, resentment, or self-defeatism, etc.

Mindfulness is the psychological exercise of bringing one, attention to situations automatically. It can be learnt through the practice of meditation and other relaxation procedures. Mindfulness has its roots in Eastern spiritual traditions like Buddhism and yoga, but it has been proven very effective by Western psychologists. It is a very common exercise and practice in America and other European countries. It is now the most valuable healing tool commonly used by clinicians and therapists. In recent years, the technique of mindfulness has become very popular in part through the work of Jon Kabat-Zinn and his Mindfulness-Based Stress Reduction (MBSR) program. Initially, it was used for cancer patients suffering from chronic pain who were taught to meditate and feel their discomfort rather than to ignore it. If it can be used for cancer patients, it can also be used for other types of patients.

Mindfulness is being applied by clinical psychologists and psychiatrists who have developed several therapeutic techniques to help those people who are facing some psychological problems and mental disorders. Mindfulness techniques have been applied to manage stress, control anxiety, reduce depression, and have proved to be useful in the rehabilitation of drug addicts. Programs based on the mindfulness practice have been applied within schools, colleges, prisons, hospitals, and many other places. It has been proven that mindfulness techniques have proved to be very useful in maintaining physical as well as mental health among normal people, critical patients, and healthy people. So, there is a positive relationship between mindfulness and human wellness. Moreover, mindfulness practice has also proved to be a preventive method for mental health problems.

While applying the technique of mindfulness, the following points are to be considered:

1. **Mindfulness is a therapeutic technique:** The technique of mindfulness is useful because it has some therapeutic values. It can be easily applied in psychiatric clinics and mental hospitals.
2. **Mindfulness focuses on the present qualities:** Mindfulness recognizes and cultivates the qualities that are usually present among human beings.
3. **Mindfulness has the potential:** This technique has a hidden potential, because it has the characteristics of being a transformative and social phenomenon. It has become a very useful technique in our modern society.

4. **Anyone can apply this technique:** The mindfulness technique is very simple and everyone can apply it and get benefit from it, and it's easy to learn. So, every person, whether male or female, can use it for their benefit.
5. **It is a part of the lifestyle:** Mindfulness is more than practice or exercise, but it is a part of a lifestyle. It brings awareness to us and helps us to know what we can do. It reduces mental and physical stress.
6. **It is evidence-based:** Mindfulness has become a scientific technique because it has been empirically proven to be useful. It is beneficial for our health, happiness, work, and social relationships.
7. **It brings innovation:** Mindfulness is an innovative technique that can help us to be effectively resilient to stressful life events and problems.

MENTAL AND EMOTIONAL WELLNESS

Human wellness consists of mental wellness and emotional wellness, which are two important components of mental health. So, here, it is essential to know about Mental wellness and Emotional wellness.

Mental Wellness: Mental wellness means that all your mental competencies are working harmoniously and functionally well. Mental wellness is related to your mental health and psychological well-being. It shows that you are intrinsically happy, healthy, and leading a prosperous life. You are content and satisfied with what you have. You don't grumble about what you do not have. You forget the past, feel satisfied with the present, and plan for your future. It gives you inner satisfaction and social acceptance. It has been suggested that mental wellness is that condition which makes it possible for the individual to face life problems in such a way as to provide him with a feeling of personal satisfaction and the welfare of the social group.

Mental wellness consists of some of the characteristics that enable an individual to meet adequately the demands of social situations. So, considering mental wellness in a social context, it may be said that mental wellness refers to social adjustment. For promoting the development of mental wellness, it is better to encourage the acquisition of attitudes, values, and habits that are important in the development of good character.

Emotional Wellness: Emotional wellness means "a positive sense of well-being which enables an individual to be able to function in society and to meet the demands of everyday life. People often link emotional wellness with positive feelings or emotions that make them feel happy and good. Emotional wellness may include contentment, enjoyment, self-sufficiency, and self-assurance in life, and the ability to cope with life's ups and downs, strains and stresses, as well as storms and struggles. Emotional wellness helps to develop satisfying interpersonal relationships with other people. It is also closely related to the social dimensions of life, or the social adjustments of individuals, which contribute to a positive state of emotional wellness.

Emotional wellness is a term that has been increasingly used in recent years. It is related to mental health and is concerned with such issues of mental disorders as stress, anxiety, and depression. Today, total health means that a person should be physically, mentally, emotionally, and socially healthy. So mental health is very much related to emotional wellness. On the positive side, enhanced emotional wellness seems to contribute to increasing coping strategies, self-esteem, good performance and productivity at work, and even longevity of life (Fredrick & Thomson, 2002). Emotional wellness also consists of two aspects of personal and social wellness, which can be assessed in terms of quality of life, the second by the evaluation of one's life in general (Kahneman & Angus, 2010).

WELLNESS Vs. WELL-BEING

The terms "wellness," "well-being," and "happiness" have often been used interchangeably by researchers, professionals, and the media. Wellness is the act of practicing healthy habits daily to attain better physical and mental health results. To know the importance of wellness, it is important to understand how it is linked to health.

Several key areas of your lifestyle are considered dimensions of total wellness. They include (i) social connectedness, (ii) exercise, (iii) nutrition, (iv) sleep, and (v) mindfulness. Each one has an impact on your physical and mental health. By making healthy practices daily, you will be well on your way towards managing stress, having positive social interactions, and achieving optimal wellness.

1. **Social Connectedness**: Good and cordial social relationships with friends or family members are a great way to help improve your physical and mental health, which will lead to human wellness.
2. **Exercise:** Even 30 or 40 minutes of daily morning walk, or jogging, or physical exercise can have a positive impact on your overall sense of wellness and help improve your physical and mental health.
3. **Nutrition**: Having a good diet and nutritious food is necessary for our living. Whereas they give energy to the body, they will help in doing daily activities actively and efficiently.
4. **Sleep**: We should plan our sleep pattern. Sleeping soundly for 6 to 8 hours at night is a must in our daily lives. We should avoid those activities before going to bed that disturb our sleep and wake us up in the morning every day.

5. **Mindfulness:** Practicing the mindfulness technique is good for the body and mind. It helps to focus and change mental functioning. It is like focusing on your thoughts, then you may become aware of how you react to stressful events. so it is better to start practicing mindfulness today.

People often confuse wellness in terms of physical health only, but it is much more than that. Wellness is a global integration of physical, mental, emotional, social, and spiritual well-being, engaging the mind and nurturing the spirit. It includes striving for health, about living life fully, and is "a lifestyle and a personalized approach to living life in a way that allows you to become the best kind of person that your potentials will allow" (Ardell 1999).

CONCLUSION

The concept of human wellness has gained significant attention in the first decade of the twenty-first century. It is related to psychological well-being, quality of life, satisfaction, and happiness. It consists of feelings of enjoyment, contentment, job achievement, and belonging. It encompasses the total mental function of an individual, as well as his adjustment to life. The concept of wellness is a dimension of behaviour, i.e., thoughts, feelings, and actions, which may enhance a sense of general well-being.

Wellness refers to physical, mental, emotional, and social health. It also includes the moral and ethical values of an individual. It consists of the way one feels about oneself, i.e., self-concept. It is concerned with the quality of his/her relationships with others and the ability to manage emotions and cope with problems. So, wellness includes both mental, emotional, and social well-being. Human wellness depends on emotional intelligence. Human wellness is generally related to economic gains, but it is also related to mental satisfaction and a peaceful state of mind, which is more stable and more productive.

Mindfulness is a new concept in human wellness. Mindfulness is the basic human ability to be aware of what we are, where we are, and what we are doing. Mindfulness also involves acceptance of the present situation, meaning that we pay attention to our thoughts and feelings.

Human wellness means the longevity of life with the absence of any kind of physical and mental illnesses and abnormalities. It is only possible if we develop a healthy lifestyle by reducing our needs and leading a simple life with some higher-level goals to be achieved. Human wellness depends upon psychic energy, which is related to an individual's emotional life.

5

MENTAL AND EMOTIONAL HEALTH

INTRODUCTION

According to the World Health Organization (2005), overall health consists of the physical, mental, emotional, and social health of a person. In our modern life, emotional health has become as important as the physical and mental health of an individual. A man should be physically fit, mentally alert, emotionally mature, and socially adjusted to lead a well-balanced life. A man who is having sound mental health will also have good emotional health, which will lead to social health. It means that all these four components of health are interrelated. It can be said that one who has good emotional health will also have good mental health.

Mentally and emotionally healthy people can adjust to their environment and solve their problems effectively and efficiently, and in this way, they get satisfaction and pleasure out of daily life. Both mental and emotional health are related to each other. It is essential to study the mental and emotional health of an individual. After reading this chapter, the readers will be able to know:

1. Nature and concept of mental and emotional health.
2. Characteristics of emotionally healthy people.
3. Importance of good emotional health.
4. Foundations of mental and emotional health
5. Improvement of mental and emotional health.

WHAT IS EMOTION?

The total health of an individual consists of physical, mental, emotional, and social health. Both mental health and emotional health are related to each other. We have already discussed much regarding mental health in the previous chapter. Here, our emphasis will be on emotional health. Before we know about emotional health, we should understand what emotion is. Crow and Crow say, "An emotion is an affective experience that accompanies generalized inner adjustment as well as mental and physiological stirred up states in the individual and that shows itself in his overt behaviour. On the other hand, Woodworth defines "Emotion is a moved or agitated state of the organism." It is a stirred-up state of feeling, i.e., the way it appears to the individual himself. It is a disturbed muscular and glandular activity, i.e., the way it appears to an external observer.

Emotion is a part of life. Every person experiences emotions in some way or another in his/her life. Emotion is the intense feelings of a person that are related to the heart. Without emotions, human beings would be little more than machines that run the same way day by day. We could not know the joys of love or the happiness of success. We could not experience sympathy for the unfortunate or grief for the loss of a loved one. Pride, envy, and jealousy would be unknown to us. Life without feeling and emotion would be drab and colorless. We all know something about emotions through our own personal and subjective experiences. Everyone is aware of anger, fear, joy, and typical human emotions. We are also aware of the importance of such feelings in our behaviour, for what we do is often motivated by them. It has great importance in human life, as we have some personal familiarity with emotions. We have all experienced fear, anger, grief, guilt, joy, love, and hate, and moreover, we have observed these emotions in others. Emotional events are complex and difficult to study.

Emotions are the primary source of human energy, aspirations, and drive, activating our innermost feelings and purposes in life and transforming them from things we think about to values we live. Emotions are subjective experiences. Emotions help us to utilize our maximum strength for short periods. Strong emotions such as fear and anger enable the organism to utilize its maximum strength.

Strong emotions tend to facilitate greater activity over prolonged periods. A person experiencing fear may be able to go for a long period without sleep. He may be able to engage in heavy physical work without experiencing fatigue. Strong emotions help us in meeting emergencies by reducing sensitivity to pain. An individual injured in an automobile accident may be completely unaware of the injury until some time after the accident has occurred. Now, it is essential to understand emotional health.

CONCEPT OF EMOTIONAL HEALTH

The concept of Emotional health is concerned with the idea of how you feel emotionally mature and relaxed in your daily life. Emotional health is related to the higher self-esteem you have. Moreover, you are usually calm and have patience with yourself and others. Emotionally healthy people have a sense of security, affiliation, and recognition with their own emotions and feelings. They do not judge others with bias and criticize others negatively without any reason.

Emotional health refers to your total psychological well-being, which includes the way you feel about yourself, the type of your relationships with others, and your ability to manage your emotions and cope with problems. An emotionally healthy person is free from anxiety, depression, or other psychological problems. Instead of the absence of mental disorders, emotional health refers to the presence of positive characteristics and personality traits.

Emotionally healthy people can adjust to their social environment and solve their problems. In this way, they help others as well as themselves and get satisfaction. Emotionally healthy people can handle life's inevitable challenges, build strong relationships, and lead productive and constructive lives. These people feel safe and secure in their own way. This is because they have learned not to judge and criticize others.

Just as physical health requires effort to build or maintain, so it is also needed for emotional health. The more time and energy you invest in your emotional health, the stronger it will be. The good news is that there are many things you can do to boost your mood, build resilience, and get more enjoyment out of life. Learning the skills required to handle emotional problems will give you a foundation of mental and emotional health.

Emotional health is related to emotional wellness, which is a part of mental health. Emotional health has many facets. Put simply, it is based on the self-esteem you feel about yourself, and the behaviour that is appropriate and healthy. So, it is based on self-prestige, self-awareness, and self-concept. It also depends on your total behaviour, which should be socially acceptable. The emotionally healthy person leads a life full of happiness and pleasurable.

NATURE OF EMOTIONAL HEALTH

The term emotional health is being used frequently these days. It may include contentment and self-assurance in life, resilience and the ability to cope with life's ups and downs, and a sense of life purpose. The capacity to develop gratifying relationships with other people is a sign of emotional health. It is closely related to the mental and social dimensions. Mental health develops in appropriate levels of independence, managing anger, stress, and conflict effectively, and communicating meaningfully with others, all of which contribute to a positive state of emotional health.

Emotional health is equated to happiness. People tend to associate emotional health with positive emotions. Emotional health is the state of consciously experiencing and accepting the existence of your feelings (joy, sorrow, fear, hate, and love. Emotional health involves managing your emotions maturely. It is a positive sense of well-being that enables an individual to function in society and meet the demands of daily life. People in good mental health can easily and early recover from illness or any other misfortune. So, emotional health is the key to a happy and healthy life.

Emotional health, in general, focuses on multiple dimensions that affect the quality of life, which leads to a balanced, healthy, and happy life. It includes both emotional and social well-being. Emotional well-being helps us to recognize, understand, experience, and express a full range of emotions and to channelize our emotions in a healthy way that satisfies our personal and social goals. On the other hand, social well-being means that an individual is well-adjusted in his environment, and he gets along with other people.

Every person, including emotionally healthy people, has problems. But emotionally healthy people can easily adjust and solve their problems. They may face some psychological problems and hazards. But they know how to tackle those problems and find their solutions easily in life. While doing so, they help others as well as themselves to get satisfaction and contentment in life.

CHARACTERISTICS OF AN EMOTIONALLY HEALTHY PERSON

Emotional health has many aspects. Behavioural skills need to be learnt to handle emotional problems, which will enhance our emotional health. Someone who is emotionally healthy exhibits the following characteristics, as outlined in the following box:

CHARACTERISTICS OF AN EMOTIONALLY HEALTHY PERSON

1. An emotionally healthy person can understand the matter and easily adapt to change. He is active and dynamic.
2. Such a person will be able to cope with stress and anxiety comfortably.
3. He will have a positive self-concept, self-image, and a positive attitude.
4. He would care for others and can give and get love from them.
5. He will be able to act independently to meet his own personal needs and demands.

The characteristics mentioned above depict the picture of an emotionally healthy and well-mature person. To be emotionally healthy, you must express your emotions in healthy ways. For example:

1. Emotional health depends upon the physical health of a person. A physically healthy person is physically and mentally fit to perform his daily routine work in his life.
2. Emotional health includes emotional well-being, which refers to a state where we can have pleasant experiences and a positive attitude towards life. He also gets enjoyment from every work that he often performs. Emotional health and emotional well-being are well-connected.
3. Most people do not have good emotional health because they are not aware of their feelings and emotions. We should educate the people regarding the virtues of having good mental and emotional health.
4. Emotional health depends upon how people judge, analyze, and evaluate their own emotions and feelings. Instead of criticizing others, we should encourage them and make them aware of their emotional health. It is better to give positive feedback to others about their emotional behaviour.
5. Like emotional health, emotional intelligence is very important in making our lives comfortable and enjoyable. Emotional Intelligence (EI) refers to the qualities of people when they are effective in interpersonal relationships and show empathetic behaviour.
6. A person possesses a high level of emotional intelligence when he is open-minded and has access to his feelings and emotions, and then his emotional health will be effective in his relationships at work or home.
7. Emotional health is the way to achieve and learn about our emotions and feelings and express them in socially approved ways.
8. An emotionally healthy person needs to learn the difference between our own thoughts and feelings and healthy emotional expression and unhealthy conditioned responses.
9. An emotionally healthy person needs to learn to feel secure with his emotions and be able to face hostile people with a smiling face.
10. Emotionally healthy people are in control of their emotions and their behaviour. They can face life's inevitable challenges and problems, build strong relationships, and lead productive and effective lives.

It is evident that incorporating relaxing exercises, such as shavasana, and utilizing stress management techniques can help us maintain happier and more relaxed lifestyles. Emotional health encompasses physical, mental, social, and spiritual well-being.

EMOTIONAL INTELLIGENCE (EI)

Emotional health is very much related to emotional intelligence. Emotional intelligence is a new concept in the field of Positive Psychology, yet it has attracted the attention of psychologists and social scientists these days. Emotional intelligence is found to be related to people's ability to manage their feelings and emotions. It's about recognizing the emotional state of ourselves and of others. EI refers to the ability to perceive, manage, and evaluate our own and others' emotions.

Emotional intelligence is a part of a person's mental and emotional health. An individual with a high Emotional Intelligence Quotient (EIQ) will naturally have better mental and emotional health. Emotional intelligence is the ability to identify, use, understand, and manage your emotions in positive and constructive ways. Some researchers suggest that emotional intelligence can be learned, developed, and enhanced. EI refers to the ability to perceive, recognize, manage, and evaluate your emotions, while others claim that it is an innate characteristic that cannot be changed, but it can only be explored and developed. To be able to change negative emotions to positive ones, one must make conscious efforts. It will help us in utilizing problem-solving techniques and to better resolve conflicts, which are the characteristics of emotional intelligence.

Emotional intelligence has, in recent years, been popularized. It is the latest development in understanding the relation between reasoning and emotion. Emotional intelligence is the most important key factor in predicting success in social and professional life. Other important factors at the place of work are technical skills, specific knowledge, mental abilities, physical fitness, physical appearance, and interest in a particular type of work, besides desires, aspirations, and career goals.

Emotional intelligence has its roots in one type of intelligence called social intelligence, first identified by E.L. Thorndike in 1920. It also referred to the Multiple Intelligence theory advocated by Gardner of Harvard University, which includes inter- and intrapersonal intelligence in his theory. Intrapersonal intelligence is the ability of a person to work covertly. It is a capacity to form an accurate model of oneself that can be used to operate effectively in life. On the other hand, interpersonal intelligence is the ability to understand other people, to get along with them, what motivates them, and how to work cooperatively with them. Emotional intelligence is a type of social intelligence that involves the ability to monitor one's own and others' emotions (Mayer & Salovey, 1993).

It has been suggested that emotionally intelligent people have better ability for problem-solving and for managing stress, more impulse control, and a more positive attitude towards oneself and others, implying greater enjoyment of life, resulting in psychological well-being. Emotional intelligence means being aware of your emotions and the ability to maintain them in control. Being able to change negative emotions to conscious awareness.

If a person has a higher EIQ, he will have good emotional health, as well as be an emotionally well-adjusted person. He will have a higher level of emotional well-being, which is the ability to appropriately recognize and regulate one's emotions for one's own well-being as well as the well-being of people around. EI is the effect of emotions on our ability to view situations objectively and thus to understand ourselves and other people. It reveals how a human person recognizes, identifies, understands, and manages his own emotions and intense feelings.

Emotional intelligence is an intelligence about being "heart smart," not just "look smart." It helps you build strong relationships, succeed at work, and achieve your goals. The skills of emotional intelligence can be developed throughout life. "EI" can be learned how to rapidly reduce stress, connect to your emotions, communicate nonverbally, use humor and play to deal with challenges, and resolve conflicts with confidence and self-assurance.

Since 1990, Peter Salovey and John D. Mayer have been the leading researchers on emotional intelligence. However, the credit for popularizing the concept of emotional intelligence goes to another American psychologist, Daniel Goleman (1995). According to the exponents of emotional intelligence, a person's emotional make-up largely determines his or her professional and personal success in life. It is now claimed that IQ may account for only about 20% of a person's success in life. The remaining 80% depends largely on a person's emotional intelligence.

The merging of emotions and intelligence as an affective and cognitive tool under the caption of EI was proposed by Yale Psychologists, Peter Salovey and John Mayer (1990). They gave definitions of EI, and the most comprehensive is the revised definition of EI in 1993. According to them, emotional intelligence involves abilities that may be categorized into five domains:

(i) **Self-awareness**, i.e., knowing your own feelings and recognizing feelings as they happen.

(ii) **Managing emotions**: It means how to handle feelings and emotions so that they are appropriate, and finding ways to cope with fears, anger, and sadness.

(iii) **Motivating oneself**: It is self-motivation or an inner motive to achieve something in life. It also means channeling emotions in the service of a goal and having self-control.

(iv) **Empathy**: It is looking to other people's feelings and emotions and appreciating how they think and feel.

(v) **Handling relationships**: It is concerned with maintaining social relationships by managing emotions in others. This component is related to social competence and social skills.

Emotional intelligence refers to the skills of emotional awareness and emotional management, which enable one to balance emotions and reason to maximize long-term competencies. Emotional intelligence includes qualities such as self-awareness, the ability to manage emotions, motivation, empathy, and social skills like communication and leadership. Emotional intelligence is the ability to know emotions and their causative factors, the capability of regulating these emotions in oneself and in others effectively. It enables a person to use emotions as a source of information for problem-solving, being creative, and dealing with social situations. So, it can be said that emotional intelligence comprises many personality traits such as empathy, motivation, persistence, warmth, and social skills.

Emotional intelligence can be either increased or minimized depending upon the type of environmental experiences one gets in one's life. The level of one's emotional intelligence is relatively measured through some tests of situations in life, resulting in one's emotional quotient (EQ), a relative measure of one's emotional intelligence. Now, some psychological tests for measuring emotional intelligence have been constructed and standardized by psychologists, which reveal EIQ. Consequently, the term emotional quotient (EQ) may be defined as a relative measure of one's emotional intelligence possessed by him at a particular period of his life.

Emotional intelligence is the product of one's heredity and its interaction with one's environmental forces. Previously, it was thought that I.Q. was the greatest predictor of success in any walk of life—academic, social, vocational, or professional. However, research conducted in the 90s onwards has replaced abstract intelligence with emotional intelligence and its measure, EIQ. They have revealed that a person's emotional intelligence, measured through these tests, may be a greater predictor of success in both personal and professional life.

IMPORTANCE OF MENTAL AND EMOTIONAL HEALTH

The maintenance of good mental and emotional health is essential to living a long and healthy life. It is seen that people who lack emotional health exhibit misfit behaviours. Their behaviours are a direct expression of their emotional health. Also, without emotional support, mental health is at risk.

According to a study done by Strine, Chapman, Balluz, and Mokdad (2010), "Inadequate social and emotional support is a major barrier to mental health relevant to the practice of psychiatry and medicine, because it is associated with adverse health behaviours, dissatisfaction with life, and disability. By receiving emotional support, your mental health can be improved and prevent mental disorders. Moral and social support systems are an asset, and those who do not have social and emotional support are more likely to develop mental disorders. This support can lead to "an increase in personal competence, perceived control, sense of stability, and recognition of self-worth, and can have a positive effect on quality of life".

People who are mentally and emotionally healthy have the following characteristics:

- They have a sense of contentment and satisfaction in their life.
- They have a zest for living and the ability to laugh and have fun. They have a keen desire for healthy living.
- They can cope with stressful situations, face an adverse environment, and bounce back from living in adversity.
- They have a sense of meaning and honesty of purpose in both their activities and their social relationships.
- They have the flexibility to learn new things and the capacity to adapt to change.
- They develop a balance between work and play, as well as rest and activity.
- They can build and maintain fulfilling and cordial relationships.
- They have self-confidence, self-efficacy, and high self-esteem.

The above-mentioned positive characteristics of mental and emotional health help us to fully participate in life, possibly through productive, meaningful activities, and we develop strong relationships with others, as well as enable us to face life's challenges and stresses. To maintain and strengthen your mental and emotional health, it is important to pay attention to your own needs and feelings. Don't let stress and negative emotions build up. Try to maintain a balance between your daily responsibilities and the things you enjoy. If you take care of yourself, you'll be better prepared to deal with challenges when they arise.

FOUNDATION OF MENTAL AND EMOTIONAL HEALTH

Our mental and emotional health is based on our interpersonal and intrapersonal relationships as well as social relationships with others. So, social interaction is very important for our mental and emotional health. Humans are social animals with many needs and demands to live gracefully in society. We also crave positive bonds with other people, i.e., friends, relatives, members of the family, peers, colleagues, and co-workers. We cannot live in isolation, as it would be like living in prison. So, the key is to find a supportive relationship with others.

So, it can be said that social interaction is the foundation of mental and emotional health. Social interaction adds charm to our lives and can help us reduce stress. We need someone who can be a good listener and support us. A good listener will listen to the feelings behind our words and will not criticize us. He will be your good friend who will give you feedback and tell you about your strong and weak points, not in the presence of other people, but in isolation, when both of you are sitting alone. You may have a few friends, but faithful and sincere ones, who want to develop a friendship with you, so that you may talk regularly and then listen to and support each other.

Strategies for social interaction with others: The following are some of the strategies that help us to have social interaction with other people:

1. **Getting time for direct relationships:** In this digital period, we sit either in front of our TV or on our computer much of the time to get the latest information about the world and related matters. Social media has also become another tool, which we use when we spend a lot of time chatting and listening to others on our smartphones. These media are useful, but they cannot take the place of our direct human relationship. Communication has become a largely pleasant experience that requires us to be in direct contact with other people, so we should not neglect our social relationships in favor of digital interaction. Despite our busy lives, we must find time to spend with our friends and relatives and exchange pleasantries.
2. **Spend time daily in face-to-face relationships**: Besides online relationships, we should also have offline and personal face-to-face relationships with our friends, colleagues, and other people with whom we come in contact daily and whose company we would like to enjoy. We should spend time with them. We should communicate with our loved ones, neighbors, and family members who are interested in us.
3. **Volunteer work:** It is better if you do some volunteer work without expecting any reward from them. It is a self-help job. It is social service and humanitarian work that will pay you later. It will give you happiness, which will enhance your emotional health. It is better if you join a voluntary agency or any social organization to do some honorary work that will provide you with pleasure and enjoyment.
4. **Join some clubs:** You should be a member of a network, social action, and special interest groups that meet regularly. You should become a member of any Social Organization, maybe the Rotary Club, Lions' Club, or Wheelchairs, etc., and do some social work. These groups provide wonderful opportunities for finding people with common interests, i.e., people you like being with whom are your good and sincere friends.
5. **Building cordial relationships:** To have good mental and emotional health, you must have very cordial and graceful relations with all those people to whom you come in contact daily. If you find it difficult to connect to others or to maintain long-term relationships,

you may benefit from reading self-help books, which are found in the academic market.

The mental and emotional health of a person depends on his emotional maturity, as the latter is a sign of emotional health. Emotional maturity is a characteristic of emotional behaviour that is generally attained by a person. A person with emotional maturity can demonstrate well-balanced emotional behaviour in his day-to-day life. A person may be said to be emotionally mature if he has in possession almost all types of emotions, positive or negative, and can express them in an appropriate degree and at the appropriate time.

CONCEPT OF EMOTIONAL WELL-BEING

Emotional well-being is one of the most important dimensions of mental and emotional health. The concept of emotional well-being has acquired more importance in positive psychology these days. Emotional well-being incorporates a holistic approach based on multiple dimensions that affect the quality of life, ultimately leading to a balanced, healthy, and happy life. It helps us to recognize, understand, experience, and express a full range of emotions and to channel our emotions into healthy behaviours that satisfy our personal and social goals. The capacity to develop cordial relationships with other people is an outgrowth of emotional well-being.

The meaning of emotional well-being is the state of consciously experiencing and accepting the existence of our feelings, i.e., joy, sorrow, fear, hate, and love at any given time. Emotional well-being involves managing our emotions with maturity. It is the positive side of well-being that enables an individual to be able to function in society and meet the demands of daily life.

A popular definition of emotional well-being has been offered by the Mental Health Foundation (WHO, 2005). According to it, "emotional well-being means a positive sense of well-being which enables an individual to be able to function in society and meet the demands of everyday life; people in good mental health can recover effectively from illness, mental disorder or misfortune." Many people equate emotional well-being with happiness. They think that to achieve emotional well-being, everybody should be happy, healthy, and prosperous in their lives. People tend to associate emotional well-being with positive emotions or emotions that make you feel happy and good. Now, psychologists have started working on the notion of happiness, because they think their main function is to make a person happy. Such happiness is usually understood in terms of contentment or 'life-satisfaction'.

Emotional well-being is a term that has been increasingly used in recent years. It is considered an individual's perceived level of happiness and satisfaction in life. However, there is a relationship between self-concept and emotional well-being, which is a part of mental health. Usually, emotionally well-being people have better ability for problem-solving and for managing stress, more emotional control, and a positive attitude towards themselves and others. It is also related to self-esteem, i.e., how we feel about ourselves and the behaviour that is appropriate and healthy. It may also include contentment, enjoyment, self-sufficiency, and self-assurance in life.

Emotional well-being and emotional health are the terms being used interchangeably these days. It also includes resilience, the ability to cope with life's ups and downs, as well as strains and stresses, as well as storms and struggles. It is related to the problems of mental health, such as anxiety, conflicts, psychological burnout, and depression, or some other mental disorder. "Evaluating our strengths and weaknesses, understanding appropriate levels of autonomy, controlling anger effectively, reducing anxiety, and resolving conflict, as well as communicating meaningfully with others, will all contribute to a positive state of emotional well-being" (Harvard Health Publication, 2010). On the positive side, enhanced emotional well-being is seen to contribute to optimism in developing coping ability, self-respect and self-prestige, self-esteem, performance enhancement at work, and even longevity of life (Frederick & Thomson, 2002).

Emotional well-being is one of the two aspects of personal well-being that can be measured in quantitative quality of life assessments, the other being 'life evaluation' (Kahneman, Daniel; Angus Deaton, 2010). It is also of interest to psychologists and other healthcare professionals. Many people equate emotional well-being with happiness and tend to associate it with positive emotions.

Emotional well-being is the state of consciously experiencing the existence of your feelings (joy, sorrow, fear, hate, and love) at any given moment. It involves managing your emotions with maturity. It helps an individual to be able to function in society and meet the demands of everyday life. So, emotional well-being is the key to a happy and healthy life. It leads to desirable social and economic results. If society regularly assesses the well-being of people, it will learn more about its causes. Emotional well-being is therefore valuable not only because it assesses well-being more directly, but it also has beneficial consequences.

There is a positive relationship between emotional well-being and human wellness. Human wellness is different for everyone, but it has a positive approach that affects the quality of life, a balanced, healthy, and happy life. Human wellness includes mental, emotional, and social wellness. Emotional well-being, which is related to mental health, helps us to identify, recognize, understand, and manage emotions for our benefit as well as for others' benefit and to channelize our emotions into socially desirable behaviour patterns and a healthy and constructive way of life that satisfies our personal and social needs.

Many people equate emotional well-being with happiness. They think that to achieve emotional wellness, everybody should be happy, healthy, and prosperous in their lives. People tend to associate emotional wellness with positive emotions or emotions that make you feel happy and good. But you cannot purchase happiness with money or wealth. You can have it or not have it, depending upon how much you are concerned about your emotional well-being.

Emotional well-being is achieved only when one is healthy in all areas of life, i.e., physically, mentally, emotionally, socially, and spiritually, where the mind, body, and soul should be in a state of balance and working together totally as a person. Well-being means a lack of illness and disease, as well as a healthy, wealthy, and prosperous life. The essentials of emotional well-being may be summed up as follows:

- Well-being gives the maximum energy for the sake of enjoyment in life.
- It gives a feeling of happiness and contentment in our daily life.
- It helps to develop skills, knowledge, and a positive attitude.
- It includes having affectionate and cordial relationships.
- It leads to a vulnerable risk of illness.
- It produces commitment, control, and challenge to be the best person in life.

Emotional well-being is achieved only when we are healthy in all areas. Total health is complete health from all angles, which includes emotional well-being.

CHARACTERISTICS OF EMOTIONAL WELL-BEING

The following are the characteristics of an emotionally well-being person:

1. **Emotional Well-being is the key to a happy and healthy life:** A person with a high level of emotional well-being must know the psychological skills that are required to face the emotional problems in life, which will help him build a sound foundation of mental and emotional health. Emotional wellness is required, especially in the period of adolescence, which is the period of change and growth, where the adolescent faces many problems of strain and stress, and the behavioural skills will help him to overcome the situation of crisis.

   Emotional well-being has many facets. It is based on self-esteem, self-prestige, self-awareness, and self-concept, i.e., how one feels about oneself. It also depends on his overall behaviour, which should be socially acceptable. The emotionally healthy person leads a life full of happiness and pleasure.

Emotionally well-being individuals also have to face some psychological problems and hazards. But they know how to tackle those problems and find their solutions easily in life. While doing so, they help others as well as themselves to get satisfaction and contentment in life. Emotionally well-being people can adjust to and solve problems.

2. **Emotional Well-being leads to total health:** Well-being means leading a life full of happiness and bliss, which is a state of optimal wellness, i.e., absence of stress, anxiety, and conflict in life. Stress management techniques require a conscious effort to lead a balanced lifestyle, doing relaxation exercises and using good coping strategies for overcoming psychological problems, developing behavioural skills for effective communication, and changing attitudes to have a happier, healthier, and enjoyable life.
3. **Emotional Well-being includes a healthy lifestyle:** There are many benefits of a healthy lifestyle. It is important to have good physical, mental, emotional, and social health.

CONCLUSION

Mental or emotional health is often referred to as overall psychological well-being. Both may include the way you feel about yourself, the quality of your relationships, and your ability to manage your feelings and emotions. Mental and emotional health isn't just the absence of psychological problems and difficulties. An emotionally healthy person is free from stress, anxiety, depression, or other psychological issues. Rather than the absence of mental disorders, mental and emotional health refers to the presence of positive characteristics.

Emotional health is defined by the degree to which you feel emotionally secure and relaxed in your daily life. It depends upon a man's emotional well-being, which is based on your self-concept and self-esteem, i.e., how you think and feel about yourself. It may include contentment, enjoyment, self-sufficiency, and self-assurance in life, resiliency, and the ability to cope with life's ups and downs and leading a life with a sense of honesty of purpose.

Emotional well-being includes the quality of our relationships, our ability to monitor our feelings, and to deal effectively with psychological problems. Emotional well-being refers to the presence of positive qualities and the development of positive attitudes. Some people need to do things that make them feel positive to achieve emotional well-being.

Emotional well-being leads to the longevity of life, with the absence of any kind of illness or abnormalities. The healthier we live emotionally, the more happiness we derive from our lives. It is only possible if we develop a healthy lifestyle by reducing our needs and desires and also lead a simple life with some higher goals to achieve. In fact, emotional well-being and emotional health are related to each other. In fact, emotional health is an important part of the totality of emotional well-being.

6

SOCIAL HEALTH—A NEW CONCEPT

INTRODUCTION

The concept of social health is a new one in this modern age. It is related to physical, mental, and emotional health, so it forms one of the four pillars of total health, i.e., physical, mental, emotional, and social. Social health is a state of psychological well-being and human wellness. It is a positive dimension of overall health.

Social health is a part of the community health service. It's about having a close relationship with family and friends and enjoying a sense of belongingness to groups. Our connections with others determine both how *well* we live and how *long* we live. Research has shown that a positive, satisfying relationship is one of the best components of health. For this reason, it is helpful to find social health as a distinct aspect that is an interconnected pillar of overall well-being.

Improving your social health can help to maintain and sustain your physical, mental, and emotional health. It means that if you nourish your body and mind but ignore your relationships, your social health may be affected, whereas a connection with others will help you to live a happier, healthier, and prosperous life. If a person is physically fit, mentally alert, and emotionally mature, then he will be socially healthy. It means that his social health depends upon physical, mental, and emotional health.

CONCEPT OF SOCIAL HEALTH

Social health is the ability of individuals to get along with other people and to form healthy and graceful interpersonal relationships with them. Social health is considered one of the pillars of psychological well-being as it relates to how comfortably you can adapt in social situations. It includes our support system for how to get through life's challenges and difficulties. It is the ability to form sincere and cordial relationships with others and to develop trust with them. This ability is closely related to our mental and emotional health.

Social health is concerned with our ability to form satisfying interpersonal relationships with others. It also relates to our ability to adapt comfortably to various social situations. These relationships should include strong communication skills and empathy for others. On the other hand, some personality traits, like withdrawal behaviour, vindictiveness, or selfishness, can affect our social health adversely. Overall, stress can also be one of the most significant threats to our healthy relationships.

Social health consists of the following characteristics, which are given in the following box:

CHARACTERISTICS OF SOCIAL HEALTH
1. Adapting to social situations, 2. Staying true to yourself in all situations, 3. Balancing your social and personal time, 4. Being engaged with others in your community, 5. The ability to develop and maintain friendships, 6. Creating boundaries in friendships and relationships, and 7. Having a supportive network of family and friends.

The above-mentioned characteristics of social health are signs that indicate strong social relationships and close bonds with other people. On the other hand, loneliness and isolation are the enemies of social health. There are several serious health effects that loneliness and social isolation can cause.

Social health also includes the network and our strong support system. Having strong interpersonal relationships indicates good social health, which emphasizes two main factors:

1. **Ability to build healthy relationships:** This includes our friends, peers, partners, family members, and professional colleagues.
2. **The quality of those relationships:** It means our ability to connect meaningfully and gracefully with other people.

Our social relationships contribute to our overall health, including social health as well as quality of life. Social health supports our mental and physical health. Research has found that poor social health is linked to many physical and mental health problems, whereas strong social connections are linked to longer life, reduced stress, and improved health. So, it can be said that social health includes: (i) maintaining healthy relationships, (ii) enjoying being with others, (iii) developing friendships and intimate relationships, (iv) caring about others & letting others care about you, and (v) contributing to society and your community.

Good personal and social relationships are the medicine for our social health. Poor social health affects us adversely and leads to social isolation, low self-esteem, stress, anxiety, depression, and other mental disorders. It can cause a variety of health issues like (i) inflammation, (ii) heart disease, (iii) high blood pressure, (iv) suppressed immune system, (v) chronic health conditions, and (vi) mental health issues. Social health supports physical and mental health.

SOCIAL FACTORS OF HEALTH

The social factors of health refer to the non-medical factors that influence a person's health. They are the wider set of forces that shape the conditions of daily life. They include social norms and social policies, as well as geopolitical systems. They are the health-promoting factors found in one's living and working conditions, rather than individual risk factors that influence the risk of a disease or vulnerability to injury. The social factors are often affected by public policies that reflect prevailing political ideologies of the land.

Social health of an individual includes the social determinants of health, which consist of the economic and social conditions that influence individual and group differences in health status (Hawe and Shiell, 2000). Social health refers to the characteristics of both society and individuals. "A society is healthy when there is equal opportunity for all and access by all to the goods and services essential to full functioning as a citizen" (Russell 1973). The social health of individuals refers to "that dimension of an individual's well-being that concerns how he gets along with other people, how other people react to him, and how he interacts with social institutions and societal mores" (Russell 1973). It bears a close relationship to concepts such as "well-being," "adjustment," and "social functioning."

The moment of social health was initiated in 1947 by its inclusion in the World Health Organization's (1980) definition of health, and by the emphasis on treating patients as social human beings who live in a complex social world. Social health has now become popular with its increasing evidence that those who are well adjusted in their communities tend to live longer and recover faster from disease. On the other hand, social isolation is a risk factor for illness. Hence, social health may be defined in terms of social adjustment and social support, or the ability to perform productive roles in society.

A satisfactory social health means good adjustment in life. Adjustment is a subjective experience and may be judged in terms of a person's fulfillment of social roles and normal social expectations. As norms vary greatly among cultures, however, a challenge lies in selecting an appropriate standard against which to evaluate roles.

Social health is also commonly viewed as a kind of social support that contributes to positive adjustment among individuals and encourages personal growth. The concept of social support underlines the theme of social health as an attribute of a society, which refers to the extent to which there is a feeling of mutual trust and reciprocity. *Social health* focuses on you and your relationships. It's something you can work on right away by improving your social skills and connecting with others. Research shows that social factors can be more important than health care or human lifestyle, which affect health.

SIGNS AND SYMPTOMS OF SOCIAL HEALTH

It is necessary to maintain our social health. Here are some signs and symptoms of what social health is:

1. **Avoid loneliness and enjoy social time:** Isolation is miserable, and social time is enjoyable. Usually, introverted people remain alone and in solitude, whereas extroverted persons may like the company of their friends. We should try to maintain a balance between loneliness and social time. In this way, we can have good social health.
2. **Be assertive but not aggressive:** Hostile aggression is not acceptable in our society, but instrumental aggression may be liked, which refers to assertiveness. It means that we should know how to communicate our needs and set healthy examples, i.e., we should not feel angry or resentful when we state our needs. We should be assertive when we put forward our viewpoints but not feel angry if we disagree with others.
3. **Be yourself:** Healthy bonds with others should make you feel comfortable in yourself. You feel a sense of belonging, meaning that you are valued, appreciated, and accepted. Friends and family members may challenge you, but you should feel relaxed so that you may not feel threatened with your sense of belonging and ego strength.
4. **Treat others with respect:** Respect others, love others, and get respect and love from others. If you're respectful, it shows that you have your social needs probably fulfilled, and you do not need to bring others down to improve your self-esteem.
5. **Have fun**: You should regularly find time for playful activities and social interaction with other people, which is a good sign that you want to maintain social health. It is better to have fun rather than frown in life.

6. **Be a part of the community:** You are a useful member of your community. It is better if you volunteer yourself at a religious or a nonprofit place, play sports, or participate in your neighborhood, which are good signs of positive social health.
7. **Have a strong social network:** You need people to work with you in emergencies and in a crisis. Good friends are those who are always ready to go out to help you. So, social health depends on friends who are there when you need them.

How to Improve your Social Well-being

Social health leads to social well-being. It's only recently that mental health has been given more importance in society. However, social well-being encompasses several aspects, including physical, mental, and emotional health, as well as Intellectual, spiritual, and vocational dimensions. While both physical and mental health are hugely important, social health greatly impacts our total health, too. Our social well-being is measured by the relationships and connections we have with others in the world around us, and social relationships help us to survive and thrive today. There are many things that you can do to improve your social health and social well-being to improve your life. For example:

1. **Practice self-care:** You should try to take care of yourself physically and mentally. You should make sure that you sleep for 6 to 8 hours daily, eat healthily, walk in the morning, exercise daily, and stop any unhealthy coping mechanisms. Meditation is also a useful mental exercise that can help you connect with yourself before connecting with others.
2. **Take things slowly:** You don't need to go for long conversations with your friends to start forming deeper social connections. You should start with small talk to practice socializing. You should ask questions about favorite TV series, hobbies, or plans for the weekend.
3. **Make the first move:** You can plan something special or have a simple tea or coffee. Seeing each other is what matters.
4. **Join a social or community group:** Group activities are a great way to meet people with shared interests. Even if you don't talk much, saying a simple "Hello" and "How are you?" can open you up to a conversation.
5. **Improve your communication skills:** This is very important. Communication skills matter a lot. Practice maintaining eye-to-eye contact, active listening, and being mindful of your body language when conversing with others. Do not lose your face value.

6. **Keep your commitment:** Control, commitment, and challenge are essential components in social relationships that can help to improve social health and social well-being.
7. **Practice gratitude:** You should try to show appreciation to your loved ones through thank-you notes, cards, or even a simple text message. Expressing gratitude goes a long way to helping others feel valued.
8. **Focus on quality connections:** Social media makes it easy to make new friends. But perceived popularity doesn't mean you have a healthy social life. It's better to focus on forming a few strong relationships with whom you can feel truly comfortable.

Social health is one's ability to create fulfilling relationships with others, develop relationships, face challenges in relationships, and the importance of communication. In this way, you can improve your social health as well as improve your social well-being.

Developing Relationships

To maintain good social health, it is essential for people to effectively develop healthy relationships. All relationships will have some level of emotional involvement, also known as intimacy. To determine how intimate a relationship will become is critical to social health. Characteristics of a healthy relationship include:

- **Trust:** One should have faith in others and will do what is best for the relationship.
- **Compassion:** One should consider others equally, as the physical and emotional well-being of others in the relationship is considered very important.
- **Respect**: Respect for each other is essential for establishing good relationships, as sacrifices made for the relationship, such as time, effort, and money, are acknowledged and valued.
- **Acceptance**: One should give and accept love and regard from others. You cannot change individual characteristics and personality traits.
- **Reciprocity**: All relationships are equal. We should believe in the give and take within the relationship.

Ways to Encourage Socially Healthy Relationships

Relationships can't be forced but think of whether it would do them good if they built their social network. Usually, socially healthy people are: (i) less stressed, (ii) more productive, (iii) healthier overall, (iv) serve the community better, (v) more creative and resilient, (vi) have more self-confidence, and (vii) are more loyal to their friends and coworkers.

1. **Celebrate events together:** We should get together around once a month to celebrate special occasions like birthdays, marriage anniversaries, milestones, and team goals.
2. **Go beyond happy hour: We should** encourage leisure time activities to get to know each other. Coffee breaks and team-building activities can bring you together in a socially healthy way.
3. **Sharing meals:** Sharing meals once a week is a great way for people to connect. If you can do it personally, consider hosting lunch on some occasion or attending lunch or dinner on some day if invited properly.
4. **Create group wellness programs:** If you can connect your group socially for a physical health program, e.g., a health checkup or eye care program, etc. Putting together a fitness and wellness program will support you in a variety of ways in a group.
5. **Set up opportunities for group gatherings:** While people in different groups may not interact often, it will help them get to know each other.

In a nutshell, keeping people socially connected with healthy relationships with others is very important. The above-mentioned points are a few ways to rebuild the important emotional aspect of health. As the need for social interaction with others is needed, your connections are meant to improve social health opportunities.

KEY POINTS

1. Social health is the aspect of psychological well-being that is related to the community.
2. Social health is an emerging concept that is different from but connected to mental health and emotional determinants.
3. While physical health relates to the body and mental health relates to the mind, social health relates to social relationships and connections with other people.

SOCIAL HEALTH AND SOCIAL INTELLIGENCE

Social health is part and parcel of social intelligence. Social health depends upon social intelligence. A person who possesses a higher level of social intelligence is considered to have good social health. The term intelligence means "intellect" and "understanding," or the ability to comprehend social situations. When we are dealing with complex facts or complex relations among facts, the comprehension of the given situation expresses our intelligence.

Social intelligence, which is a part of general intelligence, is the ability to understand and deal with people. It is the ability to get along with other people and adapt to them. It is the capacity to behave effectively in social situations. Socially intelligent people make friends easily, and they are extroverted. They also quickly understand human or social relations. It is shown in our social relationships, e.g., the diplomats, salesmen, ministers, politicians, advocates, and teachers must possess this type of intelligence.

Socially intelligent people are more successful in life, as it has been observed that many people, though they may have higher general or academic intelligence, are miserably failures in life situations on account of a deficiency in this type of intelligence.

The term social intelligence was coined by E.L. Thorndike (1920), who referred to it as the person's ability to understand and manage other people and to engage in adaptive social interactions. He noted that interpersonal effectiveness is of vital importance for success in many fields, particularly leadership. It is "the ability to understand and manage men and women, boys and girls, to act wisely in human relations". It is equivalent to interpersonal intelligence, one of the types of intelligence identified in Harvard Professor Howard Gardner's Theory of Multiple Intelligences. But Cantor and Kihlstrom (1987) redefined social intelligence to refer to the individual's funding of knowledge about the social world.

CONCEPT OF SOCIAL INTELLIGENCE

During the past few years, a lot of interest has been expressed in the concept of social intelligence. It has been highlighted in various fields today. It is the capacity of the individual to interact, with emphasis placed on interpersonal relationships in various work environments.

Thorndike (1920) had pointed out that there is an aspect of personality that can be called "Social intelligence, distinct from "concrete" and "abstract" intelligences. Guilford (1966) suggested that social intelligence could be accounted for as a fourth category of information. It implies that there are 30 abilities involved in social intelligence as specified by the structure of intellect (SI) theory, six abilities for dealing with different products of information within each of the five operations categories.

Psychologist and professor at the London School of Economics, Nicholas Humphrey, believes that social intelligence truly makes humans what they are, for example, what it is like to be a human being living at the center of the conscious present, and the sense of being an extraordinary metaphysical entity with properties which hardly seem to belong to the physical world. So, social intelligence describes the exclusively human capacity to use very large brains to effectively navigate and negotiate complex social relationships and environments.

Social scientist Ross Honey believes social intelligence is an aggregated measure of self and social awareness, evolved social beliefs and attitudes, and the capacity to manage complex social change. A person with a high social intelligence quotient (SQ) is no better or worse than someone with a low SQ; they just have different attitudes, hopes, interests, and desires.

Social intelligence is closely related to cognition and emotional intelligence. Psychologists studying social cognition and social neuroscience have discovered many principles that human social intelligence operates. Nancy Cantor and John Kihlstrom outlined the kinds of concepts people use to make sense of their social relations (e.g., "What situation am I in and what kind of person is this who is talking to me?"), and the rules they use to draw inferences ("What did he mean by that?") and plan actions ("What am I going to do about it?").

Daniel Goleman (1999) worked on social neuroscience research to propose that social intelligence is made up of social awareness (including empathy, atonement, empathic accuracy, and social cognition) and social facility (including synchrony, self-presentation, influence, and concern). According to him, our social relationships have a direct effect on our physical health, and the deeper the relationship, the deeper the impact it will have. He states that physical health affects our relationships due to the blood flow of one's body, one's breathing, one's mood, such as fatigue and depression, and can even decrease the power of our immune system.

Social intelligence is the ability to "get along with people". It was always very clear that some sort of descriptive model of social competence could be a useful resource in various aspects of human development. The concept of social intelligence is one of the key life competencies. It crystallizes much of what we know about an important dimension of human effectiveness.

Social intelligence is perhaps best understood as one of a whole range of interwoven competencies. If we can construct a model for describing, assessing, and developing social intelligence, or "SI," we can characterize SI as a combination of a basic understanding of people—a kind of strategic social awareness—and a set of skills for interacting successfully with them. A simple description of SI is the ability to get along well with others and to get them to cooperate with you.

SOCIAL HEALTH AND SOCIAL DEVELOPMENT

Social health depends upon the social development of a person. Social development is often related to the social, emotional, and personal development of an individual. This concept of social development can be stated as a combination of learning, remembering, and diplomacy to interact with an individual or a group. The social aspect of development relates specifically to the interaction of people, dependent on the different social situations that the individual is subjected to. In contrast, emotional development relates to understanding and the ability to control one's emotions. Both emotional and social development relate specifically to the internal and external progression of the individual.

The significance of social development will allow for the child's learning, relating specifically to being able to interact adequately with all types of people, whether this is family, friends, or work çolleagues. This development during the early stages of a child's life can have a huge impact on leading well-balanced and appropriate actions during the different stages of a child's existence that will lead on to adulthood, serving to define and shape the person you are.

Social development is learning the skills that help a person to interact and communicate with others in a meaningful way. Individuals communicate and interact to be able to share, talk, learn how to behave, and use appropriate language. They make friends through social development and learn how to play and have fun with others in a civilized way. Social development is the growth of a child's ability to relate to others appropriately. There are other ways to understand social development. The characteristics of social development are as follows:

1. Social development is the process of how people learn, behave, and adjust to their environment and with the people around them.
2. Social development refers to learning about interaction with the human beings around them, including relationships with others and the social skills we need to develop in our society.
3. Social development is concerned with how people can interact and communicate. It is related to having good and pleasant social skills for building good relationships.
4. Social development is how a child interacts with others, how they make friends, and builds on their social skills.
5. Social development is referred to when environmental factors affect the development of humans and change their way of living.
6. Social development is meant for establishing positive relations with others.
7. Social development is the growth of people's ability to relate to others appropriately, being trained to get along socially with others and society.

All the above characteristics of social development indicate the signs of good social health and help in developing social skills. To interact effectively with others, one must be able to monitor and control one's emotional state.

SOCIAL HEALTH AND SOCIAL MATURITY

Social health depends upon social maturity. So, it is essential to understand the phenomenon of social maturity to understand social health. Social maturity is considered an important component of one's personality. It indicates how a person reacts to the environment appropriately and adaptively. This reaction is generally learned and is not determined by one's age. Social maturity consists of being aware of the correct time and place to behave and to act appropriately, according to the situation where one lives. Social development is the process of maturity in the social behaviour of an individual. It means how a person is mature enough in his personal and social inter-relationships with others, or how he gets along with them cordially and effectively. All this affects his social health.

Social maturity means how much a person is adjusted to his social environment. A man tries to learn social adjustment from his immediate environment. Here, social maturity means the cultivation of the attitude of 'we feeling', fellow feelings, and social awareness. "Service before self' was considered the motto of social maturity. Social maturity enables a man to make positive and productive decisions during times of crisis and difficult periods. Social maturity, as described by Greenberger (1974), comprises general characteristics that represent the most common types of demands made by all societies on individuals, and at the same time, specific categories, which are culture-specific attributes of individuals that enable them to meet these demands.

Social maturity has been considered involving self-confidence, self-direction, social feeling, productivity, and social/human values. Social maturity refers to attaining maturity in social relationships, which means establishing good relations with family members, neighbors, friends, playmates, classmates, teachers, and other members of society.

According to the Advanced Learners Dictionary (2000), "Social maturity refers to the degree of growth in social and vocational abilities." According to the Dictionary of Psychology (2007), "Social maturity means social development level characterized by independence from parental and adult control in a social situation." It is characterized by the individual's ability to mix with people in social situations and manage social dealings without anybody's assistance. In other words, it is the attainment of the adult level of social behaviour after undergoing the natural process of socialization.

Social maturity implies a well-developed awareness, a deep and clear understanding of social heritage, and an appreciation of the value of social customs, manners, and more of the rules and regulations that govern social behaviour in a social group. He understands the importance of a social organization in which he lives, the desirability of rules and laws to govern group behaviour, and the overall objective and purpose of the social structure. He also develops a pattern of behaviour, habits, attitudes, manners, and skills that will help him to fit into the group living and contribute to the welfare of the group.

Social maturity is closely related to adjustment problems of school students. Socially mature students will have well-developed social abilities. The more the students are socially mature, the better their competency and ability to deal with social situations. The students who make a good social adjustment will be happy and successful. They will enjoy social contacts and live up to the expectations they hold for themselves. Social maturity among students is both a personal social problem and a concern for affected individuals, their families, and society at large.

HOW TO IMPROVE YOUR SOCIAL SKILLS

Social skills are the most important attribute of human personality and social health. Developing social skills among human beings is one of the main objectives of social health. Personality involves the inner beauty of a person. Social adjustment and social skills are the main prerequisites of one's personality. Social adjustment depends on how a person has developed his social skills.

Social skills are the ability to respond to a given situation in a manner that maintains and enhances positive interpersonal relationships. Social skill is a part of a person's total social competency, which is the overall social functioning and psychological well-being. Social competency can be improved by teaching social behaviour and social skills. It is also related to the process of socialization.

Communication as a social skill: Social skills are a group of skills that human beings use to interact with others. Communication is one of the components of social skills. Communication may be verbal or nonverbal. Verbal communication includes talking or conversations with others, sharing views, and discussing ideas which may be related to various topics like politics, current events, religion, fashion, music, technology, sports, or movies, etc. Good communication includes how effectively and impactfully you are in convincing others of your viewpoints, which shows your smartness, ingenuity, knowledge, way of expression, and the technique of presenting your ideas to others.

In non-verbal communication, your body speaks out. It includes how patient a listener you are, and secondly, how your body language works. What are your actions, reactions, and responses to others in your movements, gestures, facial expressions, etc.? Moreover, how confident you look to be in your movements, i.e., standing up straight, putting your eyes into the eyes of others while conversing. It will enhance your self-confidence, as your body language should be attuned to your verbal message.

Good communication helps a person to develop self-expression in speech, which should be fluent, flawless, and rhythmic. Self-expression will increase self-confidence, which will enhance your self-image, self-concept, self-prestige, and self-esteem. Hence, communication is one aspect of social skills that indicates good social health.

The following suggestions will serve as guidelines that help you in increasing and improving your social skills as well as your social health:

1. You should have a positive attitude towards others. A positive attitude will lead to positive thinking and positive action.
2. You should be optimistic in life. Never think of adversities likely to occur.
3. You should have pro-social behaviour. You should develop the feeling of altruism and imbibe helpful behaviour towards others.
4. If you want to have friendships with others, you may consider the good and positive qualities of others and ignore their negative points.
5. You should develop empathy in your thoughts by imbibing an accurate picture of the situation.
6. You should try to give a kind and sympathetic hearing to show that you understand the whole matter.
7. You should work with a smile and show a smiling and pleasing face to others while greeting.
8. You should show good manners while interacting with others.
9. You should be broad-minded and ignore trivial matters.
10. You may try to make peace with the past. Forget the unpleasantness of the past, face the present with reality, and think about the future rationally.
11. You should adopt the policy of forgetting and forgiving.
12. You should be very objective and not criticize others for anything.
13. You should not give adverse remarks even if you don't agree with some arguments.
14. You may ask for help when you need it.
15. You should participate in the discussion when it is being held in a group of your friends.
16. You should encourage others when it is required and praise others when it is needed.
17. You may give feedback to your friend when he is wrong and convince him without any grudge.
18. You should say some kind words in the conversation.
19. You should accept the differences and listen to them patiently.
20. You should try to resolve conflicts amicably when they occur.

The above-mentioned social skills are very useful in modifying your behaviour. They will also bring incredible effectiveness to your personal and professional life. They can add a new color of happiness and purpose to your life. They will act as motivational strategies and energize you to work increasingly in your life. You can win over friends with your pleasant manners and habits as well as lead a happy, harmonious, and prosperous social life.

CONCLUSION

Social health involves one's ability to form satisfying interpersonal relationships with others. It relates to the ability to adapt comfortably to various social situations and act appropriately in diverse settings. To develop relationships effectively and maintain good social health, individuals must be willing to develop a give-and-take policy, have adequate levels of self-esteem, and establish a sense of identity.

Social development is often related to the social, emotional, and personal development of an individual, which is concerned with social health. Social development is learning the skills that enable a person to interact and communicate with others in a meaningful way. Social development is essential for proper adjustment in society.

Social health also depends on social maturity, which means how much a person is adjusted to his social environment. It also means the cultivation of the attitude of 'we feeling', fellow feelings, and social awareness. The three dimensions of social maturity and its components are: (i) personal adequacy, (ii) interpersonal adequacy, and (iii) social adequacy. Hence, social maturity has been considered as an aggregated facet involving self-confidence, self-direction, social feeling, productivity, and social/human values.

7

MENTAL HEALTH AND POSITIVE BEHAVIOUR

INTRODUCTION

For the maintenance and upkeep of mental health, positive behaviour or positivity in life is an essential trait. Positive behaviour helps to develop love, mental peace, harmony, cordiality, happiness, and better interpersonal relationships. On the other hand, negative behaviour is responsible for creating animosity, hatred, fear, and anger among us, which adversely affects our mental health. It will make us unhappy, miserable, and sad. Positive behaviour leads to positive thinking, positive feelings, and positive actions. In contrast, negative behaviour develops negative thoughts, negative attitudes, as well as nefarious activities. Psychologists are working in this area to make the life of a man happy, effective, and successful. Positive psychologists seek "to find and nurture genius and talent and to make normal life more fulfilling" (Crompton, 2005) and not simply to treat mental illnesses. They are trying to make the world a happier place. This chapter deals with the role of positive behaviour in maintaining and sustaining the mental health of an individual.

NATURE OF POSITIVE BEHAVIOUR

Positive behaviour is concerned with positivity among human beings. It examines how people can become happier and more mentally healthy. Positive behaviour studies what makes life worth living. This type of behaviour includes the study of positive emotions, positive character traits, and positive characteristics of personality.

Positive behaviour has three main concerns: (i) positive emotions, (ii) positive individual traits, and (iii) positive personality characteristics.

1. Firstly, understanding positive emotions entails the study of making peace with the past, happiness in the present, and optimistic hope for the future.
2. Secondly, understanding positive traits of individuals consists of knowing the strengths and virtues, such as the intrinsic interest in love and work, encouragement, compassion, resilience, creativity, curiosity, integrity, self-knowledge, self-control, and wisdom.
3. Thirdly, knowing positive characteristics of personality entails the study of the values and ideals that develop better individuality and personality. Such qualities consist of justice, responsibility, civility, nurturance, work ethic, leadership, teamwork, purpose, and tolerance.

Positive Behaviour has the following objectives and tries to achieve them:

1. To allow children to flourish in their families and schools.
2. To foster satisfaction and high productivity in workplaces.
3. To encourage civic engagement in communities.
4. To identify and nurture the patients' strengths by therapists or clinical psychologists.
5. To teach positive behaviour among people.

OPTIMISM AND PESSIMISM IN POSITIVE BEHAVIOUR

Optimism and pessimism are the front and back sides of the same coin, and that coin is positive human behaviour. We usually expect good things to happen in our daily life (called optimists), while some other people think the opposite and believe that bad outcomes are likely to happen (called pessimists). According to a psychologist named Martin Seligman, who is considered the father of Positive Psychology, had studied optimists and pessimists for many years. According to him, pessimists tend to believe that bad events are the fault of some people and are an inescapable part of their lives. Pessimism puts obstacles in the way of achievement and a happy and productive life. But, on the other hand, optimists tend to believe that a bad event is just a temporary setback, and that it is due to circumstances, bad luck, or other people. They are externally oriented people. In the face of failure or other difficulties, optimists will make many attempts to overcome obstacles. As a result, they feel more in control of their lives. They believe in the external locus of control theory.

The ABCs of Pessimism: Seligman believes that an individual can learn to be more optimistic and thereby improve his or her mental health and sense of psychological well-being, though the person must learn to identify pessimistic thoughts. Seligman has developed a method for identifying a sequence of thoughts associated with pessimism that he calls the ABC method for adversity, beliefs, and consequences (Seligman, 1990).

1. **Adversity:** Anything that causes you to feel discouraged.
2. **Belief:** How you explain adversity: what I am doing here.
3. **Consequences:** The way you feel about adverse events.

The ABC method can identify a series of thoughts that will produce optimism. If your reactions to adversity consistently follow a pessimistic pattern, you can do several specific things to change your thought patterns. Seligman has outlined three useful techniques: distraction, disputation, and distancing, which are described below:

1. **Distraction**: We should begin by attempting to distract ourselves. We may slap our hand against the wall and shout 'stop'. Then we should try to think about something else.
2. **Disputation:** We should think about the adverse event. "The most convincing way of disputing a negative belief is to show that it is factually incorrect" (Seligman, 1990). The merit of this technique is that it is realistic. Learned optimism is based on accuracy, not merely on making positive statements.
3. **Distancing:** Another way of dealing with pessimistic beliefs is keeping distance. We should try to dissociate ourselves from pessimistic thoughts but try to judge the accuracy and objectivity of our thoughts. We should recognize that simply believing something doesn't make it so.

Once we have challenged our pessimistic beliefs and convinced ourselves that bad events are temporary and will not affect anything and everything we do for the rest of our lives, we will be able to look forward to better times in the future.

HAPPINESS—ASPECT OF POSITIVE BEHAVIOUR

Happiness has become a very popular topic for discussion, especially in Western countries. Michael Argyle developed the Oxford Happiness Questionnaire (Argyle & Hill, 2005) as a measure of psychological well-being. The following are some of the factors that are related to happiness:

1. **Age**: Researchers found that age affects happiness. Some psychological factors are related to happiness, as those people may live longer who are happy in their lives. Some studies have found that older individuals report more health problems, such as anger, anxiety, depression, financial problems, troubled relationships, and career stress. Researchers also recommend that people continue to do the things that bring happiness, even in old age (Vedantam, Shankar, 2008).

2. **Buying happiness:** You cannot purchase happiness with money, nor can wealth give you much happiness in life. But it is your life satisfaction or satisfaction in your personal, social, and professional life that will give you happiness. Job satisfaction is most important, which does not depend on pay, wages, or salary. It means that having money for luxuries does not increase happiness as much as enjoying one's job.
3. **Education and intelligence:** Research suggests that neither a good education nor a high IQ reliably increases happiness (Wallis, Claudia, 2005). It is assumed that IQs above 120 do not bring much happiness or success in your performances. Besides IQ level, other factors that matter more are social skills and a good relationship. One of the main benefits of intelligence and education may simply be that it allows one to reach the average level of satisfaction needed.
4. **Genetic factors:** Research indicates that genetics plays a very significant role in determining one's happiness levels. But an individual's happiness is not entirely determined by their genetics, and not even by the early life influences on those genetics.
5. **Gender:** Gender affects psychological well-being. While men report feeling less happy than women, women are more susceptible to depression.
6. **Marriage:** Martin Seligman writes that "married people are happier than unmarried people." But it depends upon individual differences.
7. **Personality:** An emotionally stable person is a happier one than an emotionally unstable person. So emotional stability and maturity go hand in hand with happiness. It also predicts higher social intelligence, which helps to manage relationships with others, which is an important part of being happy. An extroverted trait may also correlate with happiness for the same reason: it builds relationships and supports groups.
8. **Social ties:** A key aspect of successful living is healthy and strong relationships. Shenk (2009) found that health, close relationships, and how one copes with one's troubles are the main characteristics. Happiness tends to spread through close relationships like friends, siblings, spouses, and next-door neighbors, and the researchers also reported that happiness spread more consistently than unhappiness through the social network.

AREAS OF POSITIVE BEHAVIOUR

There are three broad areas of positive behaviour:

1. **Pleasant Life:** Pleasant Life, or the "life of enjoyment," investigates how people optimally experience, predict, and inculcate the positive feelings and emotions that are part of normal and healthy living. It has been considered that negative emotions can be damaging. When people experience stress, they show an increased heart rate, higher blood sugar levels, and immune suppression. If individuals are unable to regulate these changes, they can lead to illness, coronary heart disease, and heightened mortality. It has been found that positive emotions help people who were previously under stress relax back to their physiological baseline (Fredrickson et al. 2000). An improved mood is one of the various benefits of physical and mental exercise, which is cited as key to feeling happy.
2. **Good Life:** The study of the Good Life, or the "life of engagement", investigates the beneficial effects of flow state that individuals feel when optimally engaged in their primary activities. A good life means well-being and wellness, the concepts that are related to self-efficacy, personal effectiveness, mindfulness, etc. Self-efficacy is one's belief in one's ability to accomplish a task by one's efforts. Low self-efficacy is associated with anxiety and depression, and high self-efficacy can help one overcome illness easily and maintain a healthy lifestyle. High self-efficacy also improves the immune system, aids in stress management, and decreases pain (Bandura, 1977).
3. **Meaningful Life:** Investigation into the Meaningful Life, or "life of affiliation", shows how individuals derive a positive sense of well-being, belonging, meaning, and purpose of life. It involves a desire to act morally and do "good" as an emotion. Meaningful life consists of a happy and healthy life full of enthusiasm, vigor, and vitality, where one has the desire to live for a longer time.

Martin Seligman originally proposed these three areas, but has suggested that the last area, i.e., "meaningful life", be considered as one of three different categories. He articulated an account of the Good Life, which consisted of five elements. The resulting acronym is PERMA:

- P (positive) emotion–thinking every day at bedtime, three things that went well, and why.
- E (engagement)–acting by preferentially using one's highest strengths to perform the tasks which one would perform anyway.
- R (relationships)–feeling, but not in a way that can be explained briefly.
- M (meaning and purpose)–belonging to and serving something bigger than oneself.

- A (achievement or accomplishments)–determining to know what you have achieved.

IMPLICATIONS OF POSITIVE BEHAVIOUR

The practical implications of positive behaviour include helping individuals and groups to identify their strengths and use them to increase their wellness. Therapists, counselors, and many psychological professionals are using these new techniques to build upon the strengths of individuals who are having good mental health. The following points show the practical application of positive behaviour in some areas of life:

1. **Happiness in life**: It was argued that happiness is an important first step in achieving success and productivity in one's life. He promotes the achievement of happiness and positive emotions. He believes that positive psychology helps individuals to achieve their goals and to progress effectively (Sharp, Timothy, 2011).
2. **Application in education**: Positive behaviour is beneficial to students in schools as it encourages them to strive to do the best they can. According to Clifton and Rath (2005), "People believe that they work more productively when they are around positive people." Positive emotions are contagious, so having a teacher or student who is positive can help the other students to be positive and work to the best of their abilities. They believe that "positive emotions are an essential daily requirement for survival".
3. **Applications to clinical psychology:** Positive characteristics of behaviour interact with negative life events to predict disorder. Interventions that focus on strengths and positive emotions can be as effective in treating disorders as other, more commonly used approaches, such as cognitive-behavioural therapy (Seligman, Steen, Park, & Peterson, 2005).
4. **Use at the workplace**: Positive behaviour has also been implemented in business management. Furthermore, positive behaviour must be applied to an organization with transparency, as it will be welcomed by employees. Managers must also understand that the only implementation of positive behaviour will not face any commitment or challenges. However, it may help employees to be more optimistic about new concepts or management strategies.
5. **Implications for future research:** Research in Positive behaviour is also being conducted currently and applied in various countries throughout the world. For researchers to make further progress, there is a need for past theories and methods to be overcome and to encourage more contemporary research.

POSITIVE BEHAVIOUR AND MENTAL HEALTH

Mental health is very much related to the positive behaviour of an individual, as is obvious from the following points:

1. **Personal strength:** Positive behaviour, which consists of the special skills and abilities that people have, which make them unique, is called their strengths. Considering the development of these strengths, some people can help them feel more confident and have better self-esteem. In addition, it helps them express and celebrate their individuality in ways that will enable and empower them throughout life.
2. **Control:** Having control, commitment, and challenge over one's own life provides a level of confidence and self-esteem that cannot be acquired in other ways. Self-control is a sign of good mental health. Similarly, commitment to life tasks is a prerequisite, and challenges in life are a valuable element in your lifelong wellness.
3. **Philanthropy:** Philanthropy is also another important trait of our personality. One should be a philanthropist to help other people who are in crisis. To help others with donations of money, time, and other needful things during natural calamities like floods, cloud bursts, earthquakes, or other misery is considered a part of your philanthropic act. It will not only give you solace, but your actions of humanity will bring you a lot of satisfaction and contentment in life. We should learn how to be a philanthropist and acquire the value of philanthropy, which will enhance our mental health. It will also improve your self-confidence, self-esteem, and self-image.
4. **Exercise:** People should be encouraged to develop healthy habits and active lifestyles, not only improving their physical health but also their mental functioning. Physical exercise helps people learn to manage stress effectively and gives them a channel for an outlet of emotional turmoil.

Positive behaviour plays an important role, as it offers a unique perspective on mental health by showing how wellness can be improved. If you tell your mind by thinking that you are in danger (physically, emotionally, or psychologically), it reacts as if you are facing some danger. If you replace negative, irrational, self-defeating thoughts with accurate, empowering, and more adaptive thoughts, your emotional impulses will improve dramatically. It means that your social relationships with others improve, you feel in control and happy, you like and love yourself more, and you are more likely to reach your life goals. In this way, your mental health will improve positively.

ROLE OF POSITIVE THINKING IN MENTAL HEALTH

The foundation of positivism was based on a mechanistic worldview on the assumption of predictable cause-and-effect patterns of relationships. Furthermore, positivism depends on the belief that there exist some laws in the natural and social worlds that are unaffected by one's perspective. Positivism leads to positive thinking, positive attitude, and positive actions. Positive thinking leads to good mental and emotional health. So, there is a strong relationship between mental health and the role of positive thinking.

(*"See the positive side, the potential, and make an effort." ~Dalai Lama*)

POSITIVE THINKING

Positive thinking is a mental and emotional attitude that focuses on the bright side of life and elicits positive results. A person with a positive attitude anticipates happiness, health, and success, and believes that he/she can tackle any obstacle and difficulty. On the other hand, a person with negative thoughts will drain his energy and vitality. But positive thoughts can have a pleasant and blossoming effect. When you have negative thoughts, you should try to overcome them by looking internally at some beautiful and pleasant things in your mind and think of the good and pleasurable things. When we start to have negative thoughts, it is much better to shift our focus to positive thoughts. Here are ten things that can help overcome the negative thoughts that one may also try:

1. **Meditation or yoga practices:** One of the first things that one should do is yoga exercises, which will focus one's thoughts and bring attention to one's deep breathing. Yoga practice is also very relaxing, which helps to ease the mind. Yoga helps one to stay present in one's environment, as it brings one back to the now. People who meditate every day have more positive thinking than those who do not. People who meditate tend to show more **mindfulness**, or the ability to live in the present, which is also associated with positive thinking.
2. **Smile**: Smiling and laughter are very important in one's life. It helps to change one's mood and relieve stress. One should work with a smiling face and not with a frowning face.
3. **Surround yourself with positive people:** Always try to have a few friends who make constructive criticism and give you positive feedback and won't feed you with negative thinking.
4. **Change the tone of your thoughts from negative to positive**: If you have negative thinking on some days, try to change the mood from negative to positive by thinking.

5. **Take responsibility:** You are a responsible person. So, you should always think in a positive way and discharge your duties earnestly and honestly. You should not be afraid of performing truthfully and genuinely.
6. **Help someone**: You should have a helpful and cooperative attitude. Try to help others, if you can do and do something nice for another person. It will give you bliss and happiness forever in your life.
7. **Remember that no one is perfect**: You should not be idealistic, but realistic. Live on the earth and don't fly in the sky. You should know about your strengths and weaknesses. The only thing you can do now is learn from your mistakes and move forward.
8. **Music:** Music is good therapy. It acts like a catharsis, which avoids negative thinking. When we sing, we show our feelings, and this provides amazing stress relief.
9. **Write about things that seem good to you right now**: Try to write about good things that come to your mind. Even if negative thoughts come to your mind, don't shirk from writing them on paper and try to read them again. In this way, you will come to know about your weak points. In this way, you may develop positive thinking.
10. **Read positive quotes:** Write something good when you get the time. Some of the quotes may be as follows:

    Watch your thoughts, they become words.

    Watch your words, they become actions.

    Watch your actions, they become habits.

    Watch your habits, they become your character.

    Watch your character, it becomes your destiny.

Thoughts—words—actions—habits—character—destiny

Suggestions to Develop Positive Thinking

1. Positive thinking is the thought that you can change your life by thinking positively about things.
2. Positive thinking can change how you perceive it and how you react to it. And that can change the way that you feel about yourself, which can, in turn, have a huge effect on your well-being.
3. To understand the effect of positive thinking, it's helpful to think about negative thinking first. Most negative emotions, such as fear or anger, are meant to help us save ourselves from whatever is threatening us. This means that they also prevent us from being distracted by other things around us.

4. Negative thinking is not good in modern life. In the present life, when many digital advancements are happening, nobody will like your negative attitude and negative thoughts. You will only be loved by others if you possess a positive attitude and positive thoughts.
5. Negative thinking is a habit that you can train your brain to avoid. Constant negative thinking can make you much more stressed and can lead to more serious problems, like depression. So, it is better if you make a habit of developing positive thinking.

HOW TO DEVELOP POSITIVE THINKING

For developing positive thinking, it becomes essential to imbibe the feelings of positive emotions. People who think more positively are more likely to do productive things in life, as they build new skills and develop existing ones. However, positive thinking can make it easier to manage your life, reduce stress, and help you take better care of yourself. And those things are important to help you recover from serious diseases.

The most important thing is to develop good habits, e.g., write a blog focusing on positive experiences or keep a diary to write about your experiences of the past life. Moreover, it's important to make time for yourself to have fun and play for recreational purposes. Listening to music is also helpful in developing positive thinking. For developing positive thinking, it is better if you remember the following points:

1. Positive thinking is the process of creating thoughts that will create and transform your vital energy, as it is a mental attitude where you aim to get favorable results. A positive mind will bring happiness, health, and a happy ending.
2. As positive thinking is gaining popularity among us, it is better if we develop reading habits. Reading literature through good books will not only give you knowledge but also increase your vision and broaden your outlook on life.
3. A person with positive thinking will always be more successful in his personal and professional life as compared to a person with negative thinking. Many successful people will tell us that they have everything, because they have a lifestyle with positive thinking.
4. Usually, people give commands to others, "Think positive," "Don't be pessimistic".
5. We should remember the benefits of positive thinking, given below:
   (i) Reduce daily stress
   (ii) Get better health

(iii) Develop strong confidence
(iv) Live a longer life
(v) Live a happier life
(vi) Enjoy the company of your friends
(vii) Developing decision-making ability

APPLYING POSITIVE THINKING

It is better to develop positive thinking in life. For changing negative thoughts into positive ones, the following suggestions should be practiced:

1. **Use positive words when talking:** You should replace negative words with positive ones. Speak internally and silently in your mind, which is called self-talk. You should tell yourself that you can do everything in life to have a happy relationship, and you can do everything possible to have a brilliant career. It will enhance your self-confidence.
2. **Remove all the feelings that are not positive:** You should not let negative thoughts and feelings overpower you when you are in a sad mood. Even for a few minutes a day, remove negativity and focus on the positive things in your life.
3. **Use words that evoke strength and success:** You should occupy your thoughts with words that make you feel strong, happy, and in control over your life. You should try to focus on these words rather than the ones that suggest failure or incompetence.
4. **Practice positive affirmations:** One of the most common exercises for positive thinking is positive affirmation. You should start repeating a positive phrase like "I want to be happy" or "I want to be loved." If these statements are repeated, they will always impose a more positive opinion about your life and develop positive thinking.
5. **Redirect your thoughts:** This method will help you control your thoughts when you start feeling negative emotions like depression or anxiety. When you feel such emotions taking hold of you, you start generating a happy mind, a positive image, something that makes you feel better, to keep your negative feelings under control.
6. **Start thinking that you will succeed:** Always say in your mind, "I will do it, I can do it, and I will have to do it". "I will succeed; I will have to be successful." It is your self-confidence that matters a lot here.
7. **Critically analyze what went wrong:** Positive thinking does not mean that nothing can go wrong. Instead, you should analyze to

see what went wrong and why it happened, and what led to the current situation. It will work positively to avoid future mistakes and look forward with more positivity.

8. **Forgive and forget:** This is the best formula in life, i.e., "Always forget and forgive." Don't argue about things that went wrong, because it will not change anything. You should tell yourself you are forgiven and allow yourself to move on.
9. **Think of failure as an opportunity:** You should learn from your failures. Sometimes the most negative things in our lives give us opportunities that we may not have seen otherwise. For example, losing your job can be a good opportunity to open your own business or try to find another job.
10. **Working on your imagination/visualization**: Visualizing what you want to achieve or the person you want to be is a great motivation to take you there and make you think more positively about the goal that you have until you reach the destination. Have realistic dreams and try to achieve them.

You should always remember that what you live today is the result of yesterday's thoughts, and what you will live tomorrow is the result of today's thoughts and dreams. So, you should have positive dreams.

HOW POSITIVE THINKING AFFECTS SELF-DEVELOPMENT

Self-development develops skills related to positive interpersonal relationships within the family, peer groups, workplace, and community. Finding close relationships leads to the growth of self-assurance, promoting a sense of self-sufficiency. People who are encouraged to feel free to express their ideas and their feelings, such as joy, sadness, frustration, and fear, can develop strategies to cope with new, challenging, or stressful situations. It is only possible by developing positive thinking in one's life. Self-development is made up of the following aspects:

(i) **Dispositions and Attitudes**: It is about how people become interested, excited, and motivated about their learning.

(ii) **Self-confidence and Self-esteem:** It is about people having a sense of their own value and understanding the need for sensitivity to significant events in their own and other people's lives.

(iii) **Making Relationships:** It is about the importance of people forming good relationships with others and working alongside others companionably.

(iv) **Behaviour and Self-control**: It is about how people develop a growing understanding of what is right and wrong and why, together with learning about the impact of their words and actions on themselves and others.

(v) Self-care: It is about how people gain a sense of self-respect and concern for their hygiene and care, and how they develop independence.

(vi) Sense of Community: It is about how people understand and respect their own needs, views, cultures, and beliefs, and those of other people.

All these qualities can be developed if people have positive thinking.

CONCLUSION

The positive behaviour is the scientific study of the strengths and virtues that enable individuals and communities to thrive. Positive behaviour is concerned with human virtues. Positive behaviour has three main concerns: (i) positive emotions, (ii) positive individual traits, and (iii) positive personality characteristics.

There are many aspects of positive behaviour, e.g., enjoyment, contentment, buying happiness, age, gender, marriage, education and intelligence, parenting and genetic factors, personality, and social ties. These factors will help to improve the mental health of individuals. Similarly, many suggestions have been put forth for developing positive behaviours that are useful for enhancing the mental health of people. So, there is a strong relationship between mental health and positive behaviour.

Positive thinking is a mental and emotional attitude that focuses on the bright side of life and expects positive results. A positive person anticipates happiness, health, and success, and believes that he or she can overcome any obstacle and difficulty. For developing positive thinking, feelings of positive emotions will help you identify more possibilities and options in your life. They build new skills and develop existing ones, so that they genuinely have more options in life. The benefits of positive thinking are: (i) reducing daily stress, (ii) **getting better** health, (iii) strong confidence, (iv) living a longer life, (v) living a happier life, (vi) having more friends, and (vii) better management of important decisions. **Positive thinking helps in the self-development of an individual.** Psychologists have suggested some measures through which we can develop a positive attitude in our lives.

8

PROBLEMS OF MENTAL HEALTH

INTRODUCTION

This digital era, which has made our lives comfortable, has also brought misery into our lives by creating more stress and anxiety. Stress has become a part of life, but too much stress is a part of death. It has made our lives increasingly more complex and complicated. Even more needs and demands seem to have entered our daily lives. These demands have affected the mental health, wellness, and psychological well-being of people living in society. These days, many advances have been made in eradicating disease, poverty, and other problems that have plagued our society, with the strains of modern living, which have made mental illness our number one health problem. The cases of mental illnesses have also increased these days, as shown by the admission records of the mental hospitals. These conditions have given birth to many psychological problems that are related to mental health. In this chapter, we are going to study those problems.

After reading this chapter, the readers will be able to answer the following questions:

1. What are the mental health problems?
2. What are the warning signs of mental health problems?
3. What are the factors that affect mental health?
4. What are the different types of mental health problems?

CONCEPT OF MENTAL HEALTH PROBLEMS

The National Association for Mental Health estimates that one out of every two patients seeking medical aid is suffering from an illness related to mental and emotional disorders. It means that mental or emotional problems, in some ways, have contributed to the patient's illness. There are different types of mental health problems, some of which are common, such as depression and anxiety disorders, and some are not so common, such as schizophrenia and bipolar disorder (Kitchener & Jorma, 2002).

Psychological strains and stress produce some bodily complaints, sometimes imaginary, but in many other cases, emotional problems contribute to a primarily organic illness. These are called psycho-somatic disorders, which have become associated with certain bodily processes. In such cases, maladjustment or emotional difficulties are primary, and organic disturbance. It may be due to this fact that strong emotion produces widespread physiological changes throughout the body and affects the physical fitness and mental functioning of the individual.

A person may be having a mental illness if there have been changes in thinking, feeling, or behaviour for a combination of any of these causes, which are associated with distress and grief. Individuals who are seeking help for mental health problems must see a professional expert, such as a clinical psychologist or a psychiatrist, because he wants to lead a normal, happy, and contented lifestyle. Since mental health affects all aspects of a person's life, including social and physical health, work, and family relations, the importance of mental health help becomes vital. The springboard for achieving the desired mental health status is seeking the assistance of an experienced and professionally established psychologist.

The contention about mental illness seems to have been replaced by psychological well-being or wellness over the last decade of the 20th century. We may expect greater attention at the beginning of the 21st century, as our society has become more enlightened and educated regarding mental illness, which has resulted in an understanding of the prevention of mental illnesses and the preservation of mental health. Now the service of a psychologist is required, who is a doctor specializing in the treatment of mental health disorders. He will guide you into the mental freedom you seek, so long as you reach out and ask for his assistance.

WARNING SIGNS OF MENTAL HEALTH PROBLEMS

Mental health problems are widespread, but professional help from clinical psychologists or psychiatrists is also available. People with mental health problems can be treated, and many recover completely. There are many signs and symptoms of mental health problems. One or more of the following feelings or behaviours can be an early warning sign of a problem. There are warning signs that you may have a mental health problem, including:

1. Eating or sleeping too much or too little. It is better if you make a change in your eating or sleeping habits.

2. Withdrawing yourself from other people, i.e., friends, family, and colleagues, and avoiding daily activities that you would like to enjoy.
3. Having no or less psychic energy.
4. Feeling numbness in your body as if nothing has happened.
5. Experiencing aches and pains in your body without any cause.
6. Feeling helpless or hopeless.
7. Use of smoking, drinking, or drugs more than required.
8. Feeling unusually irritated, confused, forgetful, angry, upset, worried, or scared.
9. Quarreling or fighting with family members and your dear friends.
10. Experiencing severe mood swings that cause problems in your social relationships.
11. Having persistent thoughts that occur in your mind again, and that you can't get out. It is a sign of obsession and compulsive behaviour.
12. Hearing voices or believing things that are not true, hearing voices, experiencing delusions. It may be due to hallucination.
13. Thinking of harming others and yourself. It is negative thinking.
14. Inability to perform daily tasks like taking care of your children or going to the workplace.
15. Using mood-changing substances, including alcohol and nicotine, more frequently.
16. Expressing negative thinking and feelings.

If you find any of these signs in yourself, it is better to consult a psychiatrist, counselor, or clinical psychologist. Your mental health problem can be tackled, or you may overcome your mental illness and come to a normal life. But if some of the following symptoms may still occur, it may be useful to consult a mental health professional. For example:

- **Sleep or appetite changes:** Dramatic sleep and appetite changes or decline in personal care.
- **Mood changes:** Rapid or dramatic shifts in emotions or depressed feelings.
- **Withdrawal:** Recent social withdrawal and loss of interest in activities previously enjoyed.
- **Drop in functioning:** An unusual drop in functioning, at school, work, or social activities.
- **Problems in thinking:** Problems with concentration, memory, or logical thought and speech that are hard to explain.
- **Increased sensitivity:** Heightened sensitivity to sights, sounds, smells, or touch; avoidance of over-stimulating situations.

- **Apathy:** Loss of initiative or desire to participate in any activity.
- **Feeling disconnected:** A vague feeling of being disconnected from oneself or one's surroundings; a sense of unreality.
- **Illogical thinking:** Unusual or exaggerated beliefs about personal powers to understand meanings or influence events; illogical or "magical" thinking typical of childhood in an adult.
- **Nervousness:** Fear or suspiciousness of others or a strong nervous feeling.
- **Unusual behaviour:** Odd, uncharacteristic, peculiar behaviour.

One or two of these above symptoms alone can't predict a mental illness, but may indicate a need for further evaluation. If a person is experiencing several at one time and the symptoms are causing serious problems in the ability to study, work, or concentrate and relate to others, he/she should consult a physician or mental health professional.

If you just don't feel like yourself, it could be a sign you need to take care of your mental health. The following symptoms may be observed:

1. Feeling sad or down.
2. Confused thinking or a reduced ability to concentrate.
3. Excessive fears or worries, or extreme feelings of guilt.
4. Extreme mood changes of highs and lows.
5. Withdrawal from friends and activities.
6. Significant tiredness, low energy, or problems with sleeping.
7. Disrupted sleep: Poor sleep could be a red flag that you're experiencing depression or anxiety.
8. Irritability or being more emotional than usual.
9. Loss of joy.
10. Change in appetite.
11. Worsening physical symptoms.
12. Low energy.
13. Feeling sad or withdrawn for more than two weeks.
14. Severe mood swings.
15. Trying to injure or kill oneself or making plans to do so.
16. Significant weight loss or weight gain.
17. Severe risk-taking behaviour with the potential to harm self and others.

FACTORS AFFECTING MENTAL HEALTH

Many different factors can affect our mental health, including:

1. **Biological factors** or **Genetics**, such as genes, or brain chemistry, or chemical imbalances in the brain. Biological risks include genetic

factors. Gene factor is a very important factor that affects mental health. A gene has been linked to mental health disorders, such as depression or schizophrenia. Studies have indicated that variation in genes can play an important role in the development of mental problems.

2. **Psychological and personality factors:** These are specific factors that make people vulnerable to mental health problems, e.g., early adverse life experiences, such as trauma or a history of abuse. Mental health problems affect: (i) Self-esteem, (ii) result in Self-harm, (iii) Sleeping patterns, (iv) Develop stress and strains, and (v) Suicidal feelings. Your lifestyle, such as diet, physical activity, and substance use, also affects mental health.
3. **Family history of mental health problems:** Likewise, people without related genes or a family history of mental illness can still have mental health issues. Mental health conditions such as stress, anxiety, and depression may develop due to underlying life-changing physical health problems, or due to family history such as cancer, diabetes, and chronic pain. Experiences related to other chronic medical conditions also lead to mental health problems.
4. **Some other factors** which affect mental health include: (i) socio-economic conditions, such as whether work is available in the local area, (ii) occupation, (iii) a person's level of social involvement, (iv) education, and (v) quality of housing. Some other factors include: (i) gender, (ii) age, (iii) ethnicity, (iv) use of alcohol or drugs, and (v) having feelings of loneliness or isolation.

However, many other factors contribute to the development of these problems. Many other factors that contribute to mental health problems include:

1. **Risk Factors:** Risk factors for mental illness include genetic inheritance, such as parents having depression or a propensity for high neuroticism. In depression, parenting risk factors include parental unequal treatment. In schizophrenia and psychosis, risk factors include migration and discrimination, childhood trauma, bereavement or separation in families, and abuse of drugs.

   In anxiety, risk factors may include family history, temperament and attitudes, and parenting factors, including parental rejection, lack of parental warmth, high hostility, harsh discipline, high maternal negative effects, anxious child-rearing practices, drug-abusing behaviour, and child abuse, including emotional, physical, and sexual assault and violence. Several factors can contribute to the risk of mental illness. Environmental factors surrounding birth have also been implicated. Traumatic brain injury may increase the risk of developing certain mental illnesses.

2. **Social Factors:** Social influences have also been found to be an important factor, which includes sexual abuse, neglect, bullying, social stress, traumatic events, and other negative life experiences. The aspects of the community have also been implicated, including employment problems, socio-economic inequality, lack of social cohesion, problems linked to migration, and features of particular societies and cultures.
3. **Drugs:** Mental health problems are created with the use of drugs, including cannabis, cocaine, amphetamines, alcohol, and caffeine. For psychosis and schizophrenia, the use of some drugs has been associated with the development of the mental disorder.
4. **Biomedical model:** Biological psychiatry follows a biomedical model where many mental health problems are conceptualized as disorders of brain circuits, which are likely to be caused by developmental processes. It is assumed that disorders may have resulted from genetic and developmental factors. Some types of mental illnesses may be viewed as primarily neuro-developmental disorders.
5. **Electic (Bio-psycho-social) model:** Mental health problems can arise from multiple sources, and in many cases, there is no single cause that has been established. An eclectic model may be used to explain mental illnesses. The primary paradigm is said to be the bio-psycho-social model, which incorporates biological, psychological, and social factors, although this may not always be applied in practice. A distinction is sometimes made between a "medical model" and a "social model" of mental disorder.

CAUSES

Poor mental health is associated with rapid social change, stressful work conditions, gender discrimination, social exclusion, unhealthy lifestyle, physical ill-health, and human rights violations. The causes of bad mental health are as follows:

1. Poverty, which leads to:
   - (i) inferiority complex,
   - (ii) feelings of insecurity,
   - (iii) lack of self-confidence, and
   - (iv) unfulfillment of basic needs.
2. Death of one or both parents.
3. Presence of stepfather or stepmother in the family.
4. Overprotection of the child by parents.
5. Discriminatory treatment towards children.

6. Very high ideals parents put on their children.
7. Broken homes.
8. Bad Neighborhood.
9. Bad companionship.
10. Cinema and films, and TV.
11. Uncongenial school atmosphere.

TYPES OF MENTAL HEALTH PROBLEMS

There are different types of mental health problems, some of which are common, whereas others are severe but rare. Some of the problems related to mental health are given below:

I. **Anger**: Anger is a part and parcel of one's behaviour. Anger is the feeling of displeasure or resentment over maltreatment. We feel angry when we are frustrated, scared, or jealous, and sometimes, it is based on a provoking situation. Anger is a very common emotional problem among human beings. All human beings are prone to a state of anger, which affects their daily life. Anger is a negative reaction against somebody, a person, an event, or an object. It is resentment of some injustice that has been perceived to have been met. A person who perceives that something wrong has occurred usually feels anger. Anger leads to pain, which involves the physiological organs of the body.

Anger gives birth to another type of behaviour, which is called aggression, and both are often experienced at the same time. Anger is an emotion, whereas aggression is a conative behaviour. Whereas anger is internal, aggression is external. Both are typically associated with emotional and physiological arousal.

Anger may be covert or overt depending upon the situation. Covert anger may be a trait aspect of personality, whereas overt anger is considered a state anger or situational one. It may happen due to some events in the environment. State anger tends to fluctuate over time in keeping with frustration or annoyance resulting from perceived injustice, whereas trait anger is a disposition to perceive a wide range of situations. What is anger, and how to deal with it constructively and healthily?

To remain in anger for a long time leads to both psychological and physical problems. Psychologically, you spoil your interpersonal and social relationships. It affects your family and home life. Moreover, it develops excessive worry, weakens memory, creates erratic work habits, and causes sleep disorders. Physiologically, it leads to high blood pressure, increased heart attacks, depression, suicidal tendencies, and may develop psychosomatic problems.

There is every chance that such people may remain sad, become irritable and frustrated, and complain of physical and mental fatigue. They may also suffer headaches, backache, and remain under the influence of insomnia. Similarly, they develop a feeling of helplessness and hopelessness. However, managing anger is not always necessarily dangerous to health. The assumption is that anger is instinctive.

II. Anxiety and panic disorders: Stress leads to anxiety in life, which becomes a disorder if it is prolonged and persists. Anxiety disorders are the most common type of mental illness. Anxiety is a normal phenomenon, and sometimes it becomes a healthy emotion. However, when a person regularly feels severe levels of anxiety, it might become a mental disorder, as it leads to excessive nervousness, fear, apprehension, and worry. Physical symptoms, such as increased blood pressure and nausea, may also develop. Anxiety or fear that interferes with normal functioning may be classified as an anxiety disorder.

The American Psychological Association (APA) defines anxiety as "an emotion characterized by feelings of tension, worried thoughts, and physical changes like increased blood pressure." Identifying the difference between normal anxiety and a neurotic anxiety disorder will help a person to know and treat the condition. The APA describes a person with an anxiety disorder as "having recurring intrusive thoughts or concerns". Once anxiety reaches the stage of a disorder, it can interfere with daily functioning. The Diagnostic and Statistical Manual of Mental Disorders: Fifth Edition (DSM-5) classifies anxiety disorders into several main types. Commonly recognized categories include specific phobias, generalized anxiety disorder, social anxiety disorder, panic disorder, agoraphobia, and obsessive-compulsive disorder. There are several types of anxiety disorders, including panic disorder, phobias, and social anxiety:

1. **Panic Disorder:** People with a panic disorder experience regular panic attack, which involve sudden, overwhelming terror or a sense of imminent disaster, natural calamity, and death. Sudden attacks of intense terror and apprehension characterize panic disorder. These attacks can lead to shaking, dizziness, nausea, and breathing difficulties. However, a panic attack might occur for 10 minutes to an hour. Panic disorders usually occur after frightening experiences or prolonged stress. An individual experiencing a panic attack may misinterpret it as a life-threatening illness and may make drastic changes in behaviour to avoid future attacks.
2. **Phobias:** This is an irrational fear and avoidance of a particular object or situation. A person with a phobia might acknowledge fear as illogical or extreme but remain unable to control feelings of distress. There are different types of phobias:

(i) **Simple phobias:** These might involve a disproportionate fear of specific objects, scenarios, or animals.

(ii) **Social phobia:** People with social phobia often restrict their exposure to social environments. Social phobia is a fear of negative judgment from others in social situations or of public embarrassment. This disorder includes a range of feelings, such as stage fright, a fear of intimacy, and anxiety around humiliation and rejection. It can cause people to avoid public situations and human contact, making everyday living extremely difficult.

(iii) **Agoraphobia:** This term refers to a fear of situations in which getting away may be difficult, such as being in an elevator or a moving train. This is fear and avoidance of places, events, or situations from which it may be difficult to escape if a person becomes trapped. People often misunderstand this condition as a phobia of open spaces and the outdoors. A person with agoraphobia may have a fear of leaving home or using elevators and public transport.

3. **Social Anxiety or Separation Anxiety Disorder:** High levels of anxiety after separation from a person or place that provides feelings of security or safety characterize separation anxiety disorder. This is a form of social anxiety that some children experience, in which they cannot speak in certain places or contexts, such as school, even though they may have excellent verbal communication skills around familiar people.

III. Generalized Anxiety Disorder (GAD): This is a chronic disorder involving excessive, long-lasting anxiety and worries about nonspecific life events, objects, and situations. GAD is the most common anxiety disorder, and people with this disorder are not aware of the cause of their anxiety.

The American Psychiatric Association defines GAD as disproportionate worry that disrupts everyday living. People might also experience physical symptoms, including (i) restlessness, (ii) fatigue, (iii) tense muscles, and (iv) interrupted sleep. They may experience excessive anxiety in everyday situations that do not present a direct danger. The symptoms of generalized anxiety disorder (GAD) include the following:

(i) being in a high level of state.

(ii) feelings of uncontrollable worry.

(iii) increased irritability.

(iv) difficulties in concentration.

(v) problems in falling or going to sleep.

These symptoms are quite normal in daily life, though some people may experience them at persistent or extreme levels. GAD is a vague worry or more severe anxiety that seriously affects and disrupts day-to-day living.

The causes of anxiety disorders are complicated. The possible causes include:

1. **Environmental stressors**, such as difficulties at work, relationship problems, or family issues.
2. **Genetic causes**, such as people who have family members with an anxiety disorder are more likely to experience one themselves.
3. **Medical factors**, such as the symptoms of a different disease, the effects of medication, or the stress of an intensive surgery or prolonged recovery.
4. **Brain chemistry,** as psychologists define many anxiety disorders as a malfunction of hormones and electrical signals in the brain.

IV. Mood Disorders: Mood disorders are affective or emotional disorders, also known as depressive disorders. People with these disorders have significant mood changes, generally involving either mania, which is a period of high energy and elation, or a feeling of dejection or depression. Milder but still prolonged depression can be diagnosed as dysthymia. The major types of mood disorders include:

1. **Major depression:** A person with major depression experiences a constant low mood and loses interest in activities. He suffers from high blood pressure. He may feel prolonged periods of extreme sadness. A mood disorder that involves unusually intense and sustained sadness, grief, melancholia, or despair is known as major depression (also known as unipolar or clinical depression).
2. **Bipolar disorder:** A person with bipolar isorder experiences changes in his mood, energy levels, levels of activity, and ability to continue with daily life. Periods of high mood are known as manic phases, while depressive phases bring on low mood. In this disorder, both elated and grief states occur, which means both mania and depression may affect an individual. Bipolar disorder (also known as manic depression) involves abnormally "high" or pressured mood states, known as mania or hypomania, alternating with normal or depressed mood.
3. **Seasonal affective disorder (SAD):** This type of depression is related to the reduction in daylight during the autumn and winter. It changes during the rest of the year and is in response to light therapy. People who live in countries with long or severe winters seem to be affected more by this condition. Hence, it is called major depressive disorder with seasonal pattern.

4. **Post-partum depression**: After giving birth, many women experience what some people call the "baby blues." When hormone levels readjust after childbirth, mood changes can result. Postpartum depression, or postnatal depression, is more severe and may persist for months or years. There is no single cause for this type of depression.

V. Personality Disorder: Personality, which is the fundamental characteristics of a person that affects thoughts and behaviours, may be considered disordered if judged to be abnormally rigid and maladjusted. Several different personality disorders are categorized, including paranoid, schizoid, and schizotypal personality disorders; types that have been described as "emotional", such as anti-social, borderline, histrionic, or narcissistic personality disorders; and those sometimes classed as fear-related, such as anxious-avoidant, dependent, or obsessive-compulsive personality disorders.

VI. Borderline Personality Disorder (BPD): Individuals with this type of disorder exhibit characteristics of both personality disorders and mood disorders. These individuals do not remain in contact with reality and experience illusions, delusions, and other psychotic-like symptoms, such as schizophrenia, with illogical thinking and paranoid beliefs.

Individuals with borderline personality disorder are usually impulsive and unpredictable, angry, irritable, and unstable. They often experience chronic feelings of boredom and have a low tolerance for frustration. Their extreme instability is expressed in drastic mood changes and self-destructive behaviours. They typically display intense anger outbursts with little provocation and show a negative attitude. They may become verbally abusive towards their loved ones.

VII. Dissociative Disorders: Psychological dissociation is a sudden alteration in consciousness that affects memory and identity. In dissociative disorder, an individual feels isolated and becomes aloof from others. The dissociative hysterical reaction is a departure from normal states of consciousness, and it excludes certain specific activities from his daily life. Due to this, the blocking process makes it possible for the dissociative hysteric patient to be unaware of certain activities that he carries.

People who suffer severe disturbances of their self-identity and general awareness of themselves and their surroundings may be classed as having a dissociative disorder, such as depersonalization disorder or Dissociative Identity Disorder itself. Other cognitive disorders include amnesia or various kinds of old-age dementia.

VIII. Obsessive-compulsive Disorder (OCD): People with OCD have obsessions and compulsions at the same time. In other words, they experience persistent bad thoughts and a powerful urge to perform some acts repetitively, such as hand washing. It is a type of anxiety disorder primarily characterized by obsessions and/or compulsions. In this disorder, a person will often develop some superstitious thought patterns. For example, turning a light on and off a specific number of times may be employed to alleviate the obsession that something bad will happen.

A person with obsessive-compulsive disorder is subject to obsessions or compulsions. An obsession is a recurrent thought or idea that uncontrollably dominates a person's consciousness. A compulsion is an urge to perform stereotyped acts again, usually to ward off an impending feared situation. Washing of the hands again is a kind of compulsive disorder. Similarly, checking whether the door is locked or not before sleeping is another example of this disorder.

People who are abnormally unable to resist certain urges or impulses that could be harmful to themselves or others may be classified as having an impulse control disorder, and disorders such as kleptomania (stealing) or pyromania (fire-setting), or various behavioural addictions, such as gambling addiction, etc. Obsessive-compulsive disorder can sometimes involve an inability to resist certain acts, but is classified separately as being primarily an anxiety disorder.

IX. Post-traumatic Stress Disorder (PTSD): This disorder may occur after a person experiences or witnesses a deeply stressful or traumatic event. During this type of event, the person thinks that his life or other people's lives are in danger. They may feel afraid or that they have no control over what is happening. These sensations of trauma and fear may then contribute to post-traumatic stress disorder.

Anxiety and emotional experiences in the aftermath of a very traumatic event are called post-traumatic stress disorder. Individuals have painful, intrusive recollections during the day, have dreams at night, and are unable to sleep properly. They find it difficult to concentrate and feel detached from others. Acute stress disorder, like post-traumatic stress disorder, has long-lasting effects.

X. Schizophrenia: Schizophrenia is a kind of psychosis disorder and presents a serious mental health problem that affects how a person thinks, feels, and acts. People with schizophrenia may have trouble distinguishing between real and imaginary things. Schizophrenia is characterized by disordered thinking and behaviour, which often includes delusions and hallucinations. Psychotic symptoms have been experienced for at least six months, together with significant social or occupational dysfunction.

Schizophrenia is a highly complex condition whose signs typically develop between the ages of 16 and 30 years. Schizophrenia has negative and positive symptoms. Positive symptoms include delusions, thought disorders, and hallucinations. Negative symptoms include withdrawal, lack of motivation, and a flat or inappropriate mood. There are usually two types of this disorder:

1. **Schizophreniform Disorder**: It consists of the same symptoms of schizophrenia but occurs for at least one month but no more than six months. Schizotypy is a category used for individuals showing some of the characteristics associated with schizophrenia.
2. **Schizoid-affective Disorder:** It is characterized by persistent symptoms of psychosis resembling schizophrenia with additional periodic symptoms of mood (or affective) disorders. Schizoid-affective disorder has prominent mood symptoms that occur with the characteristic symptoms of psychoticism. Schizoid-affective disorder is a category used for individuals showing aspects of both schizophrenia and affective disorders.

XI. Paranoia or Delusional Disorder: It is characterized by irrational or intense fear that a person believes to be true. These beliefs may seem to be bizarre. Symptoms may last for one month or longer for a person to be diagnosed with a delusional disorder. Delusional disorder involves holding strong and false beliefs. Hallucinations are usually not present. However, under some circumstances, delusions are sufficiently false to cause problems with day-to-day life.

In this disorder, patterns of belief, language use, and perception of imaginary or real objects can become disordered. Schizotypy is a category used for individuals showing some of the characteristics associated with schizophrenia but without meeting cut-off criteria.

XII. Drug-or Alcohol-related Psychosis: Psychosis can be caused by alcohol and illegal drugs, including stimulants such as methamphetamine and cocaine. Hallucinogenic drugs like LSD often cause users to see things that are not there, but this effect is temporary. Some prescribed drugs, like steroids and stimulants, can also cause symptoms of psychosis. People who are addicted to alcohol and certain drugs can experience psychotic symptoms if they suddenly stop drinking or taking the drug to which they are addicted.

Psychotic symptoms may disappear once the effects of the substances or withdrawal symptoms occur. In some cases, substance-induced psychosis is common with stimulant drugs, e.g., methamphetamine. It explains the mental health effects of recreational drugs and alcohol, and what might happen if you use recreational drugs and have a mental health problem.

The use of drugs (legal or illegal, including alcohol), when it persists despite significant problems related to its use, may be stated as a mental health problem. The DSM incorporates such conditions under the umbrella category of substance/drug use disorders, which includes substance dependence and substance abuse. The DSM does not currently use the common term drug addiction, and the ICD simply refers to "harmful use". Disordered substance use may be due to a pattern of compulsive and repetitive use of the drug that results in tolerance to its effects and withdrawal symptoms when use is reduced or stopped.

XIII. Eating Disorders: Eating disorders involve disproportionate concern in matters of food and weight. Categories of disorder in this area include anorexia, bulimia nervosa, exercise bulimia, or binge eating disorder. Anorexia nervosa and Bulimia are the two most common eating disorders. Anorexia nervosa is a psycho-biological disease characterized by an intense fear of becoming obese, a disturbed body image, significant weight loss, the refusal to maintain normal body weight, and amenorrhea. Bulimia is an episodic eating pattern of uncontrollable food bingeing followed by purging. It is characterized by awareness that the pattern is abnormal, fear of being unable to stop eating voluntarily, depressed mood, and self-deprecation.

XIV. Sleep Disorder: Sleep disorders such as insomnia involve disruption to normal sleep patterns, or a feeling of tiredness despite sleep appearing normal.

XV. Sexual Disorder: Sexual disorders and gender dysphasia may be diagnosed, including dyspareunia and ego-dystonic homosexuality. Various kinds of paraphilia are considered mental disorders, i.e., sexual arousal to objects, situations, or individuals that are considered abnormal or harmful to the person or others.

XVI. Developmental Disorder: The developmental disorders initially occur in childhood and may be diagnosed, for example, autism spectrum disorders, oppositional defiant disorder, and attention deficit hyperactivity disorder (ADHD), which may continue into adulthood.

XVII. Conduct Disorder: Conduct disorder, if continuing into adulthood, may be diagnosed as anti-social personality disorder (dissocial personality disorder). Popularist labels such as psychopath (or sociopath) do not appear in the DSM or ICD but are linked by some to these diagnoses.

XVIII. Somatoform Disorders: somatoform disorders may be diagnosed when there are problems that appear to originate in the body that are thought to be manifestations of a mental disorder. This includes somatization disorder and conversion hysteria disorder. There are also disorders of how a person perceives their body, such as body dysmorphic disorder. Neurasthenia is an old diagnosis involving somatic complaints as well as fatigue and low spirits/depression.

XIX. Psychiatric Disorder: There are attempts to introduce a category of relational disorder, where the diagnosis is of a relationship rather than of any one individual in that relationship. The relationship may be between children and their parents, between couples, or others. They already exist, under the category of psychosis, a diagnosis of shared psychotic disorder, where two or more individuals share a particular delusion because of their close relationship with each other.

XX. Various New Types of Mental Disorder: Among those controversially considered by the official committees of the diagnostic manuals are self-defeating personality disorder, sadistic personality disorder, passive-aggressive personality disorder, and premenstrual dysphoric disorder.

CONCLUSION

The problem of mental health has become number one in the twenty-first century. These days, mental health has become our priority, as many people are facing stressful life events that cause anxiety, frustrations, depression, and many other types of mental illnesses. There are many problems with mental health programs. Psychologists are trying to solve these problems and devising some strategies and techniques to help human beings overcome those problems by managing stress and anxiety states. There are many warning signs of mental health problems. But many different factors can affect our mental health.

We can distinguish many types of mental health problems, like anger, anxiety, panic disorders, phobias, general anxiety disorders, mood disorders, personality disorders, and many more. Psychologists should consider it to be their first and foremost duty to help the mentally ill and maladjusted persons to lead as far as possible a normal life in society. Those who help in solving serious personality problems and deal with people having problems of adjustment contribute to the welfare of humanity. Perhaps this would be the greatest and finest contribution of a psychologist to mankind.

9

MENTAL HEALTH AND MENTAL DISORDERS

INTRODUCTION

Mental disorder is perhaps the major psychological problem of our modern, civilized society. However, this problem has been very much neglected in our country. Psychologists are making their best efforts to help the mentally disordered or psychologically ill people lead a happy and normal life in society. The study of mental health in the context of mental disorders may be of great value in helping the individual to adjust in life and reducing the misery that is due to mental illness, frustrations, and maladjustment in modern society.

According to a report, in America, every tenth person is suffering from some type of mental disorder or insanity, or psychological illness. These days, many people who are suffering from mental disorders are amenable to treatment and cure. In India, also, the picture is the same. Many people suffering from mental disorders seek regular guidance and counseling or treatment from psychiatrists to control the state of anxiety and overcome depression, worries, and other major or minor mental illnesses that arise out of the stresses, strains, conflicts, frustrations, and competitiveness of modern society.

NATURE OF MENTAL DISORDERS

Mental disorder is a state of mind that affects how a person feels, acts, thinks, or perceives. It may be associated with a particular functioning of the brain. A mental disorder is a negative aspect of mental health.

The concept of mental disorder falls in the perverted development of normal psychological behaviour. The maladaptive behaviour of many people who do not fit into normal forms of behaviour is known as a mental disorder. It is a deviant and unfavorable behaviour, psycho-pathologically. A mental disorder means any disorder due to a disturbance in thought, action, and feeling. "A mental disorder is the manifestation of behavioural, psychological, and biological dysfunction in a person" (DSM-IV).

Page (1976) views that the abnormal group consists of individuals marked by limited intelligence, emotional instability, personality disorganization, and character defects who, in the most part, led wretched personal lives and were social misfits and liabilities. They suffer from some type of mental disorder. Coleman (1981) holds that mental disorders or deviant behaviours are considered maladaptive because they are not only harmful to society, but to the individual. Maladaptive behaviours impair individual and group well-being, and they bring distress to the individual.

According to Diagnostic and Statistical Manual (DSM-IV, 2000), a mental disorder is a psychological syndrome or pattern, which occurs in an individual, and causes distress via a painful symptom or disability, or increases the risk of death, or pain; however it excludes normal responses such as grief from loss of a loved one, and also excludes deviant behaviour for political, religious, or societal reasons not arising from a dysfunction in the individual.

Mental disorders are serious mental conditions that may affect our thinking, mood, and behaviour occasionally. They can also affect our ability to relate to others and our daily functioning. Mental disorders are common in our society; many of us may be diagnosed with one or another in our lives. But there are methods of treatment also for cure. People with mental disorders can get better, and many of them recover completely.

Everyone has some risk of developing a mental health problem, no matter their age, sex, income, or ethnicity. Social and financial circumstances, biological factors, and lifestyle patterns may also shape a person's mental health. One study has found several socio-economic causes of mental health disorders, including poverty and living in slum areas or suburban places.

CATEGORIES OF MENTAL DISORDERS

There are many different categories of mental disorders, and many different facets of human behaviour and personality that can become disordered. A close analysis of various types of mental disorders indicates a wide range of maladaptive reactions like psychoneuroses, psychoses, delinquents, sexual deviants, and drug addicts. Thus, biological, social, and psychological maladjustment affects mental disorders, which are classified into four main categories: psychoneurotic, psychotic, mental defects, and anti-social. The following are the four main types of mental disorders:

I. **Psychoneuroses:** Page (1976) holds that psychoneuroses are relatively mild personality disorders that distress the person, but do not disrupt his social adjustments and interfere with his everyday activities. The patient does not lose contact with reality, and his personality remains intact. Psychoneurotic individuals are aware of what they are doing. They understand their mental troubles and difficulties. Their behaviour is not a source of danger to others and is rarely offensive. Such illness may or may not impair their performance.

The chief characteristic of a psychoneurotic is anxiety. Psychoneurotic reactions are the most common modes of faulty responses to the stresses, strains, and frustrations of life. Consequently, the interpersonal relationship of the neurotic becomes abnormal. Thus, psychoneurosis, in short, is a kind of mild mental disorder of which the patient is conscious. Moreover, the neurotic does not require hospitalization. Anxiety neurosis, hysteria, phobia, obsessive compulsive neurosis, etc., come under this type of mental disorder.

II. Psychoses: Psychoses is a severe form of mental disorder. The chief symptoms of psychotics involve extreme personality disorganization and loss of contact with reality and the social world. A psychotic is sharply distinguished from the normal individual by the bizarreness of his actions, the incoherence of his speech, and his general mental disorganization. A psychotic experiences hallucinations of different types, such as taste and smell, sound, and touch. His behaviour and thoughts are unaffected by logic, as it is unreasonable and inappropriate to be understood by normal people.

Thus, psychosis refers to a severe mental disorder that disintegrates personality and disrupts the individual's interpersonal as well as social relationships. Psychotic patients are usually hospitalized, as they are unable to take care of themselves. They become a danger and threat to the welfare of society by creating disturbances, being hostile, and violent.

A psychotic distorts reality and becomes disoriented towards people and things in the external world. He has no proper idea or knowledge of time and place, which makes his personality increasingly disordered. Without any apparent reason, he becomes suddenly excited, depressed, violent, and irritable. In short, there is permanent impairment of total personality. A psychotic's behaviour is colored by delusions when he claims to be an emperor, a big cinema star like Amitabh Bachan, a multi-millionaire, or above all God.

Schizophrenia is the most common form of psychotic disorder, having paranoid reactions and characterized by "breakdown of integrated personality function, withdrawal from reality, emotional blocking, distortion and disturbances of thought and behaviour" (Coleman, 1974).

III. Mental Retardation: The mentally deficient are also called feebleminded or mentally defective. Those whose IQ is less than 80 degrees on any intelligence test are called mentally retarded children. With training and guidance, they may show some improvement, but up to a limit after which they do not gain or learn from training, instruction, or education.

Mentally retarded children consist of severe (idiots), moderate (imbeciles), and mild (morons) mental retardation. In such cases, low levels of intelligence have been there since birth, and such types do not significantly indicate any brain disease.

Mental retardation is called mental sub-normality and mental disability. Such children are known by so many names other than mentally retarded, such as mentally handicapped, mentally deficient, mentally sub-normal, or mentally sub-average, etc. It connotes the sub-average mental functioning of a group of children, which affects not only their behaviour and future development but also creates serious problems for the people responsible for their welfare.

Mental retardation is a serious disability. Children with intellectual disability need special assistance to learn. Their learning problems also create obstacles in other areas of life. With support from families, friends, teachers, and peers, mentally retarded students can be successful in school and lead happy and productive lives like others. The mentally retarded child is not benefit from normal classroom teaching and finds no motivation in classwork.

IV. Anti-Social Personalities: The anti-social personalities are divided into two parts: (i) law violators, and (ii) individuals with psychopathic personalities. The law violators are again classified from the legal point of view into (i) delinquents, and (ii) criminals. A minor who commits an offence is a delinquent in the eyes of the law. A small portion of the criminals are mentally defective, but most of them have average and sometimes superior mental ability. Now they are called socially ill or maladjusted people.

Anti-social personality disorder is characterized by "a pervasive pattern of disregard for, and violation of, the rights of others that begins in childhood or early adolescence and continues into adulthood." Psychopaths and sociopaths are related to anti-social personality disorder, called Dissocial personality disorder.

Psychopath was the term used for a personality disorder characterized by an abnormal lack of empathy combined with strong amoral conduct but marked by an ability to appear outwardly normal. Later, the name of this mental disorder was changed to Anti-social Personality Disorder. It encompasses anti-social, psychopathic, and sociopathic personalities. However, some researchers have stated that anti-social personality disorder is diagnosed via social deviant behaviours, whereas a diagnosis of psychopath also includes affective and interpersonal personality. In fact, psychopaths and sociopaths are two distinct kinds of anti-social personality disorder.

SIGNS AND SYMPTOMS OF MENTAL DISORDERS

Several signs and symptoms indicate a mental disorder. While every mental illness is different, here are seven common signs of a mental disorder:

1. Change in feelings
2. Loss of interest
3. Change in sleeping patterns
4. Low psychic energy
5. Difficulty in interacting with others
6. Weight changes and appetite loss
7. Unmanageable emotions

The following are five warning signs of mental illness to watch for, especially when you have two or more of these symptoms, which means that you are suffering from a mental disorder.

1. Excessive fear, worry, or anxiety
2. Long-lasting sadness or irritability
3. Extreme changes in moods
4. Social withdrawal
5. Dramatic changes in eating patterns

Mental health conditions can also begin to develop among young children and adolescents. Because they're still learning how to identify and talk about thoughts and emotions, their most obvious symptoms are behavioural. Symptoms in them may include the following:

- Changes in school performance
- Excessive worry or anxiety, for instance, fighting in class
- Hyperactive behaviour
- Frequent nightmares or fearful dreams
- Frequent disobedience or aggression
- Frequent temper tantrums

Each mental disorder has its own symptoms, but common signs of mental illness in adults and adolescents can include the following:

- Excessive worrying or fear
- Feeling excessively sad or low

- Confused thinking or problems concentrating and learning
- Extreme mood changes, including uncontrollable "highs" or feelings of euphoria
- Prolonged or strong feelings of irritability or anger
- Avoiding friends and social activities
- Difficulties understanding or relating to other people
- Changes in sleeping habits or feeling tired and low energy
- Changes in eating habits, such as increased hunger or lack of appetite
- Changes in sex drive
- Difficulty perceiving reality (delusions or hallucinations)
- Inability to perceive changes in one's own feelings, behaviour, or personality
- Overuse of substances like alcohol or drugs
- Multiple physical ailments without obvious causes (such as headaches, stomach aches, vague "aches and pains")
- Thinking about suicide
- Inability to carry out daily activities or handle daily problems and stress
- An intense fear of weight gain or concern with appearance

CAUSES OF MENTAL DISORDERS

The following are some of the causes of mental disorders:

1. **Mental Causes:** Many etiological factors which cause mental disorders are grief, worry, fear, remorse, fright, and disappointment in love or the death of a relative. Large numbers of cases have been attributed to such causes. Some psycho-pathological predisposition must determine these unfortunate consequences. Many factors, like deep-rooted conflicts in personal life, may be some of the mental causes.
2. **Economic Factors:** Poverty, unemployment, underemployment, overpopulation, child labor, and the hundreds of other economic factors that increase the burden of living for the poor are often contributing factors in the causation of mental disorders.
3. **Preventive Measures:** The enormous increase in the burden of studies for the school students puts pressure on mental life, which is the early recognition of those factors that endanger mental health. Education must be fundamentally altered to fit the needs of children and those with special difficulties. So disastrous are

the results of failure to make the modifications in teaching that these children require. The whole educational system might well be examined with reference to their special needs. It will prove to be the trigger for preventive measures.

DIAGNOSIS OF MENTAL DISORDERS

Psychiatrists and clinical psychologists provide a medical diagnosis of mental disorders for the patients through the assessment of signs and symptoms associated with particular types of mental disorders. The majority of mental health problems are initially assessed and treated by physicians or a family doctor during consultations, who may refer a patient on for more specialist diagnosis in acute or chronic cases.

Routine diagnostic practice in mental health services typically involves an interview known as a mental status examination, where evaluations are made of behaviour, self-reported symptoms, mental health history, and current life circumstances. Sometimes, the use of psycho-metric tests is also conducted as a standardized diagnostic criterion, and in rare special cases, neuro-imaging tests may be requested. The views of other professionals, relatives, or other third parties may be considered. A physical examination to check for ill health or the effects of medications and other drugs may be administered. More structured approaches are being increasingly used to measure levels of mental disorders.

PREVENTION OF MENTAL DISORDER

The 2005 WHO report "Prevention of Mental Disorders" stated that "Prevention of these disorders is one of the most effective ways to reduce the disease burden." The 2011 European Psychiatric Association (EPA) guidance on prevention of mental disorders states, "There is considerable evidence that various psychiatric conditions can be prevented through the implementation of effective evidence-based intervention programs. In India, the 1982 National Mental Health Program included prevention, but implementation has been slow, particularly of prevention elements.

A standard way of preventing any mental disorder is psychological counseling. This can include cognitive-behavioural therapy (CBT), psychotherapy, or a combination of therapies. There are ways to reduce the risk of mental disorders. The following steps should be taken to help moderate mental illnesses:

- Reduce caffeine, tea, cola, and chocolate.
- Before using herbal remedies, check with a doctor or pharmacist for any chemicals that may make anxiety symptoms worse.

- Maintain a healthy diet.
- Keep a regular sleep pattern.
- Avoid alcohol, cannabis, and other recreational drugs.

TREATMENT OF MENTAL ILLNESSES

Treatment for mental disorders is based in psychiatric hospitals or in community clinics, where assessments are carried out by psychiatrists, clinical psychologists, and clinical social workers, using various methods but often relying on observation and questioning. Treatments are provided by various professional experts. Psychotherapy and psychiatric medication are two major treatment options. Other treatments include social interventions, peer support, and self-help.

While any mental disorder, like anxiety, can cause distress. In an anxiety state, some alarms become noticeable through a raised heartbeat, sweating, and increased sensitivity to surroundings. These alarms cause a rush of adrenaline, a hormone and chemical messenger in the brain, which triggers these anxious reactions in a process called the "fight-or-flight' response.

There are various methods for tackling mental health problems. Some strategies or treatments are more successful in combination with others. A person living with a chronic mental disorder may make different choices at various stages in his life. The individual needs to work closely with a psychiatrist and a clinical psychologist who can help him identify his needs and provide him with suitable treatment. Treatment of any mental disorder will consist of a combination of psychotherapy, behavioural therapy, medication, counseling, etc.

1. **Psychotherapy:** This type of treatment takes a psychological approach to treating mental disorders. Cognitive behavioural therapy, exposure therapy, and dialectical behaviour therapy are some of the examples. Psychiatrists, clinical psychologists, psychotherapists, and some professional experts carry out this type of treatment. It can help people understand the root of their mental illness and start to work on healthier thought patterns that support everyday living and reduce the risk of isolation and self-harm.
2. **Medication:** Some people take prescribed medications, such as antidepressants, antipsychotics, and anxiolytic drugs. Although these cannot cure mental disorders, some medications can improve symptoms and help a person resume social interaction and a normal routine while they work on their mental health. Some of these medications work by boosting the body's absorption of feel-good chemicals, such as serotonin from the brain. Medicines that might control some of the physical and mental symptoms include antidepressants, benzodiazepines, tricyclics, and beta-blockers.

(i) **Antidepressants:** These are commonly used medicines which help with anxiety, even though they also target depression. People often use serotonin reuptake inhibitors (SSRI), which have fewer side effects than other antidepressants but they are likely to cause nausea and sexual dysfunction when treatment begins. Other antidepressants include fluoxetine, or Prozac, and citalopram, or Celexa.

(ii) **Benzodiazepines:** A doctor may prescribe these for certain people with anxiety, but they can be highly addictive. These drugs tend to have few side effects except for drowsiness and possible dependence. Diazepam, or Valium, is an example of a commonly prescribed benzodiazepine medicine. But benzodiazepines have the most serious warning from the Food and Drug Administration (FDA). A warning alerts doctors and patients about drug effects that may be dangerous. Only take benzodiazepines as your doctor prescribes. Talk with your physician if you have any concerns about safely taking this drug.

(iii) **Tricyclics:** This is a class of drugs older than SSRIs that provide benefits for most anxiety disorders other than OCD. These drugs might cause side effects, including dizziness, drowsiness, dry mouth, and weight gain. Imipramine and clomipramine are two examples of tricyclics.

(iv) **Beta-blockers:** Additional drugs a person might use to treat anxiety include: (a) monoamine oxidase inhibitors (MAOIs), (b) beta-blockers, and (c) buspirone. Seek medical advice if the adverse effects of any prescribed medications become severe.

3. **Self-help/Self-treatment:** A person coping with mental health problems may need to make changes to his lifestyle to facilitate wellness. Such changes might include reducing alcohol intake, sleeping more, and eating a balanced, nutritious diet. People may need to resolve issues with personal and social relationships that may be causing damage to their mental health. People with mental disorders may benefit from relaxation techniques, which include deep breathing, meditation, and mindfulness. There are several exercises and actions to help a person cope with their psychological problems, including:

   (i) **Stress management techniques:** Learning to manage stress can help to control strain and stress in life. Exercise, like progressive relaxation techniques, may help lessen your anxiety and other mental problems, so that you may have a balanced and stress-free life.

(ii) **Relaxation techniques:** Simple daily activities can help soothe the mental and physical signs of anxiety. These techniques include meditation, deep breathing exercises, long baths, resting in the dark, and yoga.

(iii) **Exercises to replace negative thoughts with positive ones:** Make a list of the negative thoughts that might be troubling and write down another list next to it containing positive, believable thoughts to replace them. Creating a mental image of successfully facing a specific fear can also provide benefits for anxiety symptoms related to a specific cause, such as a phobia.

(iv) **Support system:** Talk with supportive and familiar people, such as a family member or friend. Support system services may also be available in the local area. Social and moral support is very important.

(v) **Exercise:** Physical exercise can improve self-image and release chemicals in the brain that trigger positive feelings.

4. **Counseling**: Counseling is done by a psychologist who is an expert in counseling. It can change harmful thought processes that form the foundation of troublesome feelings. In the process of counseling, it is hoped that the distorted thinking will be changed and that they will be able to judge how they react to objects or situations that trigger mental problems. For example, a psychotherapist providing counseling for panic disorders will try to reinforce the fact that panic attacks should not give heart attacks. This encourages people to confront their fears and helps reduce sensitivity to their usual causes of mental disorders.
5. **Breathing**: Breathing is a useful but relaxing technique that aims to return breathing to its normal rhythm. The breathing exercise may help to focus the mind, relax the body, and improve concentration. The technique is known as "resetting your breath," which is easy to do, quick to learn, and can be a highly effective technique for people in stressful situations. Breathing is a simple technique that a person can do anywhere or in any setting. Before starting, people should sit with their backs supported in a comfortable chair and their feet on the floor. They can use the following method:

   (i) Close your eyes. Breathe in through your nose while counting to five slowly. Feel the air enter your lungs.

   (ii) Hold your breath inside while counting slowly to five. Do not shut your mouth or nose. Simply try inhaling or exhaling for five seconds.

   (iii) Then begin slowly exhaling for five seconds.

   (iv) Repeat steps 1 to 3 at least five times.

Once someone is used to this technique, he may choose to count to six to eight times. Breathing can help to positively affect emotions and mental well-being, and wellness. Resetting one's breath or working to make the breath leave fight-or-flight mode is good for both the mind and body. In fight-or-flight mode, the body feels threatened and reacts to help the person escape or avoid a threatening situation. The body also releases hormones to make the heartbeat faster, and breathing quickens and boosts blood sugar levels. People with high-stress jobs, such as soldiers and police officers, often use breathing when their bodies are in fight-or-flight mode. This technique is also relevant for anyone interested in improving their concentration.

Benefits of Breathing: Breathing may provide several benefits to those who do it. The following are four benefits of breathing:

1. **It reduces physical stress symptoms in the body:** The Deep breathing technique has been shown to significantly reduce the production of hormones associated with stress, such as cortisol.
2. **It affects positive emotions and mental well-being:** The use of breathing techniques can be helpful in the reduction of stress, anxiety, and depression.
3. **It increases mental clarity, psychic energy, and focus:** Breathing exercises could bring about better focus and a more positive outlook. Participants can manage impulses, such as those associated with addictive behaviours. Moreover, it will increase your psychic energy.
4. **It improves your reactions to stress:** Breathing may have the ability to change someone's reactions to stress. It has been suggested that "relaxation response" practices, such as meditation, deep breathing, and yoga, can alter how the body reacts to stress by changing how certain genes are switched on.

Once someone experiences the physical, psychological, and emotional benefits of breathing, he will want to do it daily. There are several steps that people can take to make breathing easier:

1. It is better to find a quiet space to begin with breathing. A person can do this anywhere, but it is easier if there are fewer distractions.
2. With all deep breathing techniques, placing one hand on the chest and another on the lower stomach can help. When breathing in, try to feel the air and see where it is entering.
3. Focus on feeling an expansion in the stomach, but without forcing the muscles to push out.
4. Try to relax the muscles instead of engaging them.

With only four steps, mastering deep breathing is possible for anyone looking to add more consciousness and relaxation to their daily routine. Deep breathing is one of many breathing techniques that can be useful in the reduction of day-to-day stress. Breathing has been proven to be a powerful tool in managing stress, regaining focus, and encouraging positive emotions and a state of mind.

Breathing techniques like deep breathing are one of the easiest to master, which are commonly used to increase alertness and achieve calmness, including: (1) Pranayama breathing, (2) Alternate nostril breathing, (3) Meditation breathing.

CONCLUSION

In these days of technological advancement and scientific growth, mental illnesses and mental disorders are increasing day by day due to the hectic hustle and bustle of modern life. The mental health program has become the order of the day. We must understand the nature of mental disorders occurring daily in our lives. We should be aware of the symptoms, causes, and etiological factors that contribute to mental abnormalities among human beings. It should be accepted beyond doubt that abnormality is perhaps the major problem of a modern civilized society. It is, however, unfortunate that this problem has been very much neglected in India.

Psychologists have also done work on the treatment of mental disorders. Treatment includes psychotherapy, medication, self-help techniques, counseling, and breathing exercises. Stress management techniques, relaxing exercises, negative thinking stoppage, and a social support system, besides doing physical exercises, have become very essential these days to lead a happy and prosperous life.

10

FRUSTRATION AND CONFLICTS IN MODERN LIFE

INTRODUCTION

Every man is born with some needs, both physiological and psychological. When an infant comes into this world, his/her first need is feeding, getting milk from the mother, so he/she cries to tell the mother that he/she is hungry and needs milk. The physical needs consist of hunger, thirst, sleeping, to keep rest when tired, to wear clothes according to weather demand, to save himself from the vagaries of weather, and when he grows up, the biological need of sex arises. Similarly, we have psychological needs such as to seek love and affection from others, to get recognition, and a craze for achievement, need for belonging or affiliation, as well as a need for security, etc. It is not possible to have all needs fulfilled in our lives.

A person remains busy throughout his life to fulfill his needs; some of them remain unfulfilled, which creates problems. Some needs are fulfilled, while others are thwarted. Then he continues to solve his problems. When he is unable to solve the problems, which puts some pressure on his mind, it results in strain and stress. Stress creates anxiety, which leads to tension in one's life. It is the cause of frustration in life; when our needs are not fulfilled or thwarted, the outcome is frustration. You lose your peace of mind and are unable to concentrate on your work and perform well.

Our mental health is concerned with how well we are adjusted in our social environment. So, it becomes essential to understand what we mean by maladjustment. When you feel that you are unable to cope with the realities of life and unable to face the challenges in the environment, you feel maladjustment, which is a minor mental disorder. All these are psychological problems that need to be solved if you want to lead a peaceful, balanced, and harmonious life. In this chapter, we will discuss the details regarding frustration, conflicts, and maladjustment. Lastly, we will also narrate some techniques of defense mechanisms which may help a person to overcome these critical conditions and give solace to their troubled life.

FRUSTRATION

Frustration is a very troublesome and torturous mental condition. Frustration may be caused by mental conflicts, which are often produced. When you are unable to decide on a matter or if you lack the decision-making ability to solve your problems, which are often created in your life. Frustrations and mental conflicts that make your life miserable will make you maladjusted. It is all related to the problem of adjustment and maladjustment in life. First, we should study what frustration is.

The term 'frustration' refers to the conditions that fail a need or motive to be satisfied. When the satisfaction of the needs is thwarted, because we do not always reach the goal that we aspire to, the interference with goal-directed behaviour is often known as frustration. Another common cause is the conflict of motives. If the individual wants two goals at the same time, he is likely to experience a great deal of discomfort and stress before making a choice. Anxiety, tension, strains, and other emotional disturbances are the symptoms of frustration.

Man's behaviour is goal-directed. The motivational behaviour, which is directed towards certain goals, is thwarted and remains unsatisfied. The satisfaction of the motive involved is blocked, and then frustration is caused, which is the internal state of emotional disturbance. This thwarting or interference with goal-directed behaviour is known as "Frustration".

The incidence of frustration is greater among human beings in complex and industrialized societies. In a competitive society, where the chances of failure are increased, the probability of frustration is also increased. A need or motive must be present for frustration to occur. Interference with the satisfaction of motives is only one of the many sources of frustration. Another common source is the conflict of motives. A conflict situation evokes two or more motives, the satisfactions of which are incompatible. An individual cannot fight against his conflict directly, as he can against his simple frustrations.

Throughout our lives, we face situations in which we are unable to satisfy our motives completely. Most of the situations in life call for adjustment, i.e., for persistent activities directed towards the achievement of goals in the face of difficulties. But sometimes, when a person is unable to reach his original goals, the needs persist, and individuals do not usually give up their goals entirely but adjust.

Sources of Frustration: Any object that interferes with the satisfaction of some perceived needs creates frustration and leads to inner tension and stress. There are mainly two major sources of frustration:

(i) External environment in the form of barriers or obstacles.
(ii) Internal—within the organism in the form of deficiencies of one type or another.

1. **External Environment**: The external sources of frustration may be either physical or social. Lack of various things can be equally frustrating. Frustration caused by social sources begins almost as soon as we are born. In fact, the process of socialization inevitably leads to frustration. Physical obstacles in your environment, e.g., your car breaks down when you are going to a scheduled meeting, you feel tension, which will cause frustration.
2. **Internal:** Frustration is sometimes caused by internal factors that prevent satisfaction of certain motives within the organism. The deficiencies in the form of physical handicaps may be extremely frustrating to the affected individual. Personal characteristics such as an unattractive appearance, low intelligence, and physical weakness can be sources of frustration. It leads to inner tension and stress.

REACTIONS TO FRUSTRATION

There are individual differences as far as their reactions to frustration are concerned. Some people have little ability and capacity to overcome even the routine type of life's frustrations, while others have a lot of tolerance and patience to face frustrating situations. They appear to have an unlimited capacity for overcoming all obstacles. There are two types of reactions to frustrative situations.

Adaptive vs. Non-adaptive Reactions

1. **Adaptive reactions** that involve the process of adjustment, which represent direct ways of dealing with the problem. In this type of situation, people try to modify, change, or remove the objects that cause frustration.
2. **Non-adaptive reactions** involve distortions of reality aimed at defending oneself against anxiety. They are not directly oriented towards changing or removing frustrating situations.

Direct Adaptive Reactions: There are three general types of direct adaptive reactions. For example:

(i) Attack and aggression
(ii) Flight and withdrawal
(iii) Compromise and substitution

1. **Attack and aggression:** The usual first response to frustration is an aggressive attack on the person or thing that caused it. It is a negative form of reaction. Aggression of this type is not liked and strongly discouraged in our society, because physical attack on somebody else may prove to be fatal. It may result in punishment and further frustration. Aggression faces punishment or disapproval, which is replaced by a fearful and insecure attitude. Such a person may respond to frustration not only with aggression but also by a conflict between his impulses for aggression and his fear of retaliation.
2. **Flight and withdrawal:** When aggressive behaviour is not liked or it has not led to the elimination of the frustrating situation, a person may flee from the situation, which is withdrawal behaviour, i.e., fight or flight state.
3. **Compromise and substitution** represent adequate reality-oriented modes of response in some frustrating situations.

CONFLICTS

Conflict is a common phenomenon and frequently occurs in a person's life. Conflicts may be minor and resolved easily, and some of them may be major, which are resolved with great difficulty. For example, a young lady going to a dance party must choose one between two attractive dresses, a student who must choose one subject out of two offered subjects, i.e., mathematics and biology subjects at the same time; a young executive who has been offered a promotion wants the higher salary but shirks from the additional responsibilities. Hence, conflicts underlie most instances of maladaptive behaviour. There is a relationship between conflict and frustration.

Conflict has been defined as a situation in which two or more incompatible behaviour trends are evoked that cannot be satisfied fully at the same time. According to the field theory of behaviour developed chiefly by Kurt Lewin, a well-known psychologist, conflict can be described in terms of the interactions between an individual and his environment. It emphasizes the observation that behaviour does not depend on the organism alone or on the environment alone, but on what goes on between the two.

Decision-making ability is required when there is mental conflict. Among the various types of conflicts, decision-making ability has the most significant quality. A young man may have to decide out of the conflict when he may choose freely between two offered positions. A child may have to decide between reading an interesting book and going out to play in the ground. A young woman who lacks the decision-making quality is having a mental conflict between two equally qualified matches for her wedding occasion.

Decision-making is a cognitive ability that is related to the reasoning power of an individual. We may have many big problems which we face in everyday life where much more important decisions have to be taken, e.g., what type of school to go to, which job to accept, what type of house to buy and in which locality, whether to continue or end a long-term relationship with somebody very close to you, etc. If you have the ability for rational thinking and decision-making, you would like to make each of these decisions in a cool, calm, and rational way. In this way, you will overcome the conflicts occurring in your life while trying to solve those problems.

The decision-making process also involves a problem-solving activity, which gives a solution considered to be correct and satisfactory. It is therefore a process that is based on rational thinking. It can be said that the decision-making process is the skill of selecting one appropriate line of action between two or more choices. Moreover, the process of decision-making involves choosing between possible alternatives to a problem. Decisions can be made either through logical or illogical reasoning, or a combination of the two. It can be stated that decision-making is the process as well as the action of making important decisions in day-to-day functioning in professional, personal, or social life.

In many cases, we are simultaneously attracted to two mutually exclusive goals with positive attractive value. When the two goals look equal in attractiveness, the length of the vacillation period increases, and the conflict is produced. The prospective medical student who must choose between going for marriage or joining a medical college makes his decision quickly if one goal is substantially more attractive to him than the other. Another student faced with choosing between two difficult courses may entertain the idea of selecting some other course.

Man has to face many conflicting situations in life as life has become very complex. He is in the process of solving the various types of problems that he faces, but he is unable to solve all of them. Conflict comes in the way of solving his problems, especially when he faces frustrations and maladjustment. He must adjust, but he is unable to do so.

Behaviour tendencies may be represented by vectors, which show the direction and strength of the individual's striving. Most impulses can be described as directed towards or away from environmental events. This is stated in terms of values. Positive values are tendencies to approach, and negative values are tendencies to withdraw and avoid. The interaction of the individual with the situation brings either positive values or negative values, as it may be perceptible from the following Figure:

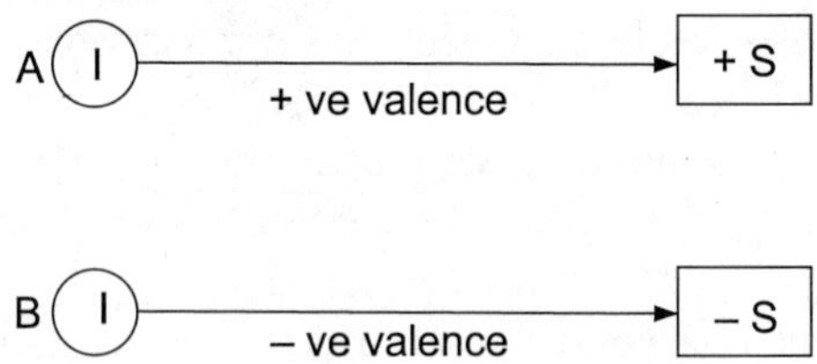

In the above Figure, in A, the interaction of the individual (I) and the situation (S) may be described as a positive valence, in B as a negative valence (After K. Lewin).

Conflicts are not only the precipitating causes of adjustive difficulties but also have a relationship to the ability to adjust when confronted by new problems. Many experiments show that strong, unsolved, early conflicts make enduring changes in personality. If a person persists over a period of years in making inferior, excessive, or non-adjustive responses, some devastating influences may have probably reduced his general ability to adjust.

MALADJUSTMENT

Throughout life, everyone experiences frequent thwarting, failures, and disappointments while trying to satisfy his needs and desires, which create conflicts in his mind. An individual has many needs and desires, some of which are in harmony with reality, while others are incapable of being attained. If he can do so, he gets well-adjusted to life situations. But if he fails to do so, mental conflicts may develop, and he may feel maladjusted.

In their lives, all living human beings meet situations in which they cannot achieve their motives promptly or completely. A college student faced by the competitive activities of other students may not be able to achieve much prestige, approval, or success. All these situations demand adjustment, i.e., for persistent activities directed towards the realization of goals in the face of difficulties. When a person is unable to reach his original goals, he does not usually give up his motives entirely but makes adjustments.

Most individuals have a desire to attain great wealth or to become extremely popular, but hardly any few of them attain these. Those who take their failures realistically become satisfied with what they have attained and can be said to be well-adjusted individuals, but those who are always cursing themselves for their failures or who adopt abnormal means to satisfy their needs for power or wealth by illegal means are the people who have a maladjusted personality.

All of us have many needs and desires that conflict with each other, because they are themselves contradictory or they cannot be achieved at the same time. These conflicting situations that are faced in a socially approved manner reduce the tension. Those situations may be dealt with in two ways: (i) an ineffective method when the individual may do anything, still the conflict is not resolved, and (ii) an undesirable method when the individual reacts in such a manner that he apparently resolves the conflict and at least temporarily reduces the tension.

Most individuals adopt effective techniques for dealing with many conflicting situations, but there are a few individuals who resort to a mode of response that is ineffective or undesirable. Those who fail to resolve conflicts adequately are maladjusted individuals. Physical factors such as glandular imbalance, chronic disease, or physical weakness are also responsible for maladjustment. Similarly, bad environmental influences adversely affect the individual's personality. It is also noted that a very large number of maladjustments are directly caused by too many conflicting situations.

The manifestation of maladjustment may occur in the form of aggressive behaviour, withdrawal, or nervous habits, such as bullying, stealing, truancy, disobedience, defiance, intolerance, destructiveness, and temper tantrums. Examples of withdrawing behaviour are shyness, fearfulness, daydreaming, unsociability, and secretiveness. Tics, nail biting, fidgeting, and thumb-sucking are varieties of nervous habits. Hence, it can be said that maladjustments are due to the failure of an individual to adjust properly by the removal of conflicts and the reduction of tensions.

Methods of Adjustment and Tension Reduction

Adjustments are of various types, as shown by different individuals. These adjustment methods vary widely in the effectiveness with which they reduce the tensions aroused by conflicting situations. The most effective methods of tension reduction involve the individual consciously attempting to reduce the tension. A few important methods of adjustment are discussed below:

Direct Methods of Tension Reduction and Adjusting: Direct methods are those in which the individual consciously tries to reduce the tension, such as:

1. **Destroying or removing the barrier:** The most direct response to a goal that is blocked is an attempt to destroy or remove the barrier.
2. **Seeking another path:** When the individual fails to remove the barrier, he is likely to seek another path to the goal.
3. **Substitution of other goals:** If attempts to reach the original goal fail, the person may consider another suitable goal. The substitute goal reduces the tension; it compensates for that need that has been thwarted by the original goal. In our life situations, we often substitute goals, e.g., a student who wishes to be a professor in

college substitutes this goal with that of being a teacher in high school if he is unable to get a placement in any college.

4. **Analysis and decision:** When a person is confronted with two or more equally desirable but contradictory goals, there are relatively few alternatives. He may renounce one of the goals, or he may renounce both goals, and he may try to work out a compromise between them.

   The individual in such cases follows the method of problem-solving in achieving the goal and consequently can decide which goal to accept. Sometimes, an individual, instead of renouncing one goal and accepting the other, obtains a solution that arrives at a compromise between these two. This is also helpful in tension reduction.

Indirect Methods of Tension Reduction and Making Adjustment: Indirect methods are primarily meant for avoiding or reducing tension, pain, and distress brought about by thwarted needs. In some instances, they may serve to prevent an action which would result in distress, in others to restore feelings of security or adequacy.

Indirect methods of tension reduction are often known as defense mechanisms. They are typically unconscious and are concerned with the immediate removal of distress. It may be possible that these mechanisms may reduce the tension now but may complicate the problem so much as to make long-term adjustment more difficult to achieve.

Substitute Adjustments: They are meant to cope with the tensions of their basic motives. They give indirect or partial satisfaction to strong motives and hence tend to reduce tension. It is driven by an intense urge to satisfy one particularly strong need; it may end by thwarting other equally important motives. Similarly, constructive adjustments can be made as a result of more frustration, which may result in better adjustments than conflict, and a strong emotional reaction to difficulties is detrimental to good adjustment.

DEFENSE MECHANISM

The defense mechanism is the non-adaptive reaction of an individual against frustrating situations. Sometimes reactions involve distortions of reality that are meant not to solve the problem but simply to protect us against tension. Such non-adaptive reactions are adjustive mechanisms, which are called defense mechanisms, that are observed in the behaviour of every human being. In our culture, adjustment mechanisms are needed to cope with feelings of defeatism, failure, and an inferiority complex. They tend to defend an individual against recognition of his inadequacies. For this reason, they are called defense mechanisms.

Some of the important defense mechanisms which have great significance in the adjustment process of the individual are: (i) Rationalization; (ii) Repression; (iii) Projection; (iv) Identification; (v) Regression; (vi) Substitution; (vii) Sublimation; (viii) Compensation; (ix) Reaction formation; (x) Withdrawal; and (xi) Daydreaming. The description of some of the defense mechanisms is given below:

1. **Rationalization:** Rationalization is the most used technique in our daily lives. In this technique, we try to rationalize our behaviour and justify our actions, whether they are right or wrong. Even if we try to justify our mistakes or wrongdoings. When we rationalize, we find logical but false reasons for past, present, or future behaviour. We put those reasons which protect us from admitting our weaknesses and shortcomings. It occurs on an unconscious level. To serve as a protection against anxiety, defense mechanisms are always employed without our conscious awareness. We always try to justify the actions that we have made and will make our wrong actions seem right ones.

   People may defend themselves by words or thoughts as well as by actions. They justify their behaviour by giving socially acceptable reasons for it, which they have learned to regard as inferior or shameful. These rejected motives may include the aggressive impulses directed towards frustrating circumstances and people. A student may try to justify by some lame excuses for not achieving good grades in his final examination. He may blame his teacher for his revengeful attitude. A dancer may blame his surroundings for not performing well (*Nach na jane angan teda*).

2. **Repression:** This concept occupies a central position in the Freudian school of psychology. According to Freud, anxiety is one of the kinds of pain leading to and causing repression. The examples may be lapses of memory, slips of tongue, or pen, etc. Thoughts and impulses that conflict with the social values of an individual are unpleasant and troublesome. Even thinking about them results in unpleasant feelings of guilt and anxiety. Consequently, an individual may adjust by inhibiting his responses to these needs and by forgetting them in his conscious awareness. Then these thoughts go into the unconscious mind. But these repressed responses do not remove the motives; they merely keep them from being recognized and satisfied. The basis of repression is the phenomenon of inhibition.

   Aggression and sexual impulses cause considerable difficulty in our society. Repressed aggression may lead to some psychological problems, like alcoholism or psychosomatic illness. Hypertension is believed to result from repression of aggression, which is recognized as a symptom of severe intrapsychic tension caused by the inability to express aggression. Here, it is important to see how much repression has occurred and what type of material has been repressed.

On the other side, suppression is regarded as conscious and voluntary, while repression is thought of as unconscious and involuntary. Forgetting is largely unmotivated, while repression is motivated. The forgotten material is largely unrecoverable, while repressed material may be recovered or brought to consciousness through hypnosis, psychotherapy, and other techniques.

3. **Projection**: Projection means blaming others for your wrongdoings. "Projection involves the reference of impulses, thoughts, feelings, and wishes originating in the person himself to persons and objects in the outside world" (Symonds, 1949). All of us have a tendency to save ourselves from our weaknesses and limits. We have difficulty in seeing ourselves as others see us. We tend to emphasize our strong points and overlook our shortcomings. "One way of doing this is to project these attributes into others." We try to project our weaknesses onto others by blaming them. A student who has been caught cheating in the examination may try to project his feelings that other students were also cheating.

   A person tries to condemn such faults strongly, but he expresses his own guilt and self-condemnation indirectly rather than recognizing his own shortcomings. Projection is especially noticeable in sexual conflicts. It is seen mostly in delusions of persecution. Feeling thwarted, the individual has an impulse to attack the sources of his frustration aggressively.

4. **Identification:** In identification, we try to identify ourselves with other people. A clerk may try to identify himself with his close relative who is a big officer. A lower division clerk who hides his inferior feelings will try to talk about his uncle or some other relatives who are in high positions. Instead of his own achievements, he will tell the achievements of his relatives. When we identify, we assume certain characteristics of an admired person. There are two things involved in this mechanism:
   (i) Modeling: To model the behaviour of the most popular person.
   (ii) An individual who attempts to live out his wishes in the life of another person.

   Identification can provide a person with ambitions, ideals, and goals; a sense of security, but it can lead to dissociation from real life. Life satisfaction can be gained through the accomplishments of other people. Identifications can also develop outside the family group and act as adjustments to individual social groups. Sometimes we try to identify ourselves with some hero in the films that we see or in the novels that we read.

5. **Regression:** In regression, a person behaves like a younger person. When an adult acts like a child to avoid that situation. When he starts weeping like a child to save himself from an ugly situation, to avoid the penalty for his wrongdoings. It means that he has gone to the regression stage. Here, one reverts to a type of behaviour appropriate to a younger age. It may be viewed as a reaction to some difficult and frustrating situation. These are two types of regression:

   (i) Retrogression and (ii) Primitivizing

   (a) Retrogression involves reverting to a type of behaviour once actually manifested by the individual.

   (b) Primitivizing involves a change from mature behaviour appropriate to the age of the person involved to immature behaviour.

   Regression means to revert to solutions that were satisfying at an earlier period of personal development. When an older person starts behaving like a small child, it means that he has gone into a phase of regression.

6. **Substitution:** It refers to the replacement of certain unapproved or unacceptable impulses or feelings with those that are approved and accepted. For a successful adjustment to life, there must be a mechanism, i.e., a means of healthy substitute satisfaction. A girl who aspires to be a doctor in her future life and is unable to achieve her goal may substitute her goal by becoming a nurse in the hospital. A person who wants to be a professor in college may substitute his goal by becoming a lecturer in the school.

7. **Sublimation:** An adolescent must sublimate his surplus psychic energy into useful and socially desirable activities. Sublimated impulses are those impulses that are a substitute for the original or natural expression of an impulse, and which are, at the same time, harmonious with the original impulse, which is socially acceptable. When the sex instinct is channelized into the socially approved exhibition of pictures, models, or some other artistic creation, it is called sublimation. A painter tries to sublimate his libido energy by exhibiting pictures of sexual aberration. A creative writer tries to sublimate his sexual desires by writing a short story or composing a poem exhibiting his unfavorable impulses.

Sublimation is a substitute response that is socially acceptable and does not interfere appreciably with the satisfaction of other motives. Aggressive responses to thwarting are sublimated into interests in participation and spectator sports. Aggressive behaviour is channeled by boxing in the playground. This is called instrumental aggression.

8. **Compensation:** If you are unable to achieve something in one area, you will try to achieve it in some other area. This is called compensation. It is generally described as an "attempt to overcome a subjective shortcoming in one area of activity by excelling in some other area." Anxiety feelings that arise from failure in an activity may lead to increased attempts to excel in some other activity. Compensation refers to the tendency to excel in areas in which the individual feels inferior and which, for him, causes tension. When a physically disabled child is unable to participate in outdoor activities, he will try to excel in studies by achieving excellence in academic accomplishments. It is compensatory behaviour. Usually, it is seen that a physically handicapped student who is unable to participate in sports will try to excel in studies.

   Compensatory behaviour consists of an excessive display of a characteristic to balance or conceal deficiency. It covers a great variety of specific forms of behaviour. Children have especially strong needs for compensatory adjustment due to their greater dependence on others. Normally, they achieve this goal through aggressive play. Adults also have their normal compensation that helps them relieve the humdrum of ordinary existence. Parents often seek compensation through the accomplishments of their children. It is an externally oriented type of substitute adjustment. A person who could not become an IAS officer in his lifetime will aspire to achieve it through the accomplishments of their children. This is compensatory behaviour.

9. **Reaction formation:** In some cases, when impulses generate tension, the individual defends himself by giving strong expression to the opposite feelings. The individual is unaware of his true feelings and generally manifests behaviour that is exactly the opposite. In some cases, the individual is reacting against somewhat feminine personality characteristics. If one is severely criticized or punished for acting unmanly, then the manly impulses or interests may arouse some doubt, and that person would like to behave like a woman. We sometimes react to the opposite of what is happening. Sometimes, reaction formation is an exercise for attracting the attention of others.

10. **Seclusiveness or Withdrawal:** An escape mechanism, withdrawing, timid, or seclusive behaviour is very direct evidence of a fearful response to social situations. This is a flight action. Withdrawing avoids failure by not attempting to place himself in competition with others; so, it has a substitute adjustive value, but it provides no satisfaction for the person's continuing social needs. It usually results in attitudes of self-condemnation and anxiety. When a person withdraws from some social situation due to some physical or mental deficiency, it is called withdrawal behaviour. Everyone shows the seclusive adjustment to some extent, especially when in a new situation in which normal adjustive satisfactions have not been established. A habitually seclusive person is difficult to readjust, because he has not acquired the skills in dealing with people that most people use in their social contacts.
11. **Fantasy or Daydreaming:** Daydreaming is both an escape and a compensatory mechanism. It is also one technique of a defense mechanism. A person can imagine any of the satisfactions of objects that he does not attain more directly in his lifetime, including professional success, money, wealth possessions, sex satisfactions, intellectual brilliance, physical strength, beauty, and other goals towards which he strives. This is a universal source of adjustive satisfaction. Fantasy occurs frequently in cases with markedly seclusive adjustments and is meant for tension reduction. It is like a fanciful delusion that has positive value in invention, literature, and art. An adolescent girl usually dreams of leading a very luxurious life after marriage, but later falls prey to an ordinary type of life.

CONCLUSION

Mental health consists of adjustment, and adjustment is a lifelong process. When a person is unable to adjust, he feels frustrated in life. When the satisfaction of the needs is thwarted, because we do not always reach the goal that we aspire to, the interference with goal-directed behaviour is often known as frustration. Everyone inevitably experiences frequent thwarting, failures, and disappointments while seeking to satisfy his needs, impulses, and desires. It leads to frustration and conflicts in life. Frustration may be due to any cause that leads to mental health problems. There are adaptive and maladaptive techniques to cope with frustrating situations. Another common cause is the conflict of motives. One of the causes of maladjustment in life is conflict, which is the state of inability to make decisions. Conflicts can also be resolved with defense mechanisms that have great significance in the adjustment process of the individual.

11

PROBLEM OF SUICIDE IN OUR SOCIETY

INTRODUCTION

Suicide is a mental health problem among young people, which has become a very serious problem in our society. Its incidence is increasing day by day due to depression among people. It is self-murder. Suicidal behaviour refers to a mental disorder that is caused due to various factors. When a person thinks of dying or does not want to live in this world, he will commit suicide. Suicide means ending his own life with the help of a method. Thoughts of committing suicide may be considered a psychiatric problem, and a psychiatrist should be consulted to help such a person to come out of the negative thoughts.

Suicide is a psycho-social and mental problem. It is related to the mental and emotional health of a person. It deals with intra-personal relationships and involves social consequences. Suicide is an act of intentionally causing one's own death. Because it is a self-injurious behaviour with the desire to end one's own life, it is a criminal offence. So, for mental health professionals, it is their main duty to save them from taking such drastic action.

SUICIDE—A MENTAL HEALTH PROBLEM

Suicide is a major mental health problem that has a fatal outcome. It is an act that is performed deliberately by a person who is under depression. The word 'suicide' has been derived from the Latin word 'suicidium'. Here, '*sui*' means oneself, and '*cidium*' is killing. So, this word means killing oneself, and so it is an act of committing suicide for the purpose of killing oneself to die and ending one's life. A suicidal attempt is when someone harms himself with the intention of ending his life.

Failed suicide is a non-fatal suicidal behaviour that is caused by self-injury or harming oneself with the intention to end one's life, but it does not result in death. It is an attempt to commit self-murder. There is a tendency to die when thoughts about death take place. It means that negative thoughts occur in the mind of a person when he becomes insane. In normal conditions, a person desires to live and to lead a happy life. But under abnormal conditions, he will go for committing suicidal attempt. Sometimes, a person murders another person out of anger to take revenge for some reason and then commits suicide to escape arrest and face the murder trials. This is a case of extended suicide. Due to some family problems, a person may murder his wife or children before committing suicide.

When a person is in acute pain and suffering that has become unbearable, or when he is unable to find some other method to escape from the misery in his life, he thinks it is better to die than to lead a miserable life. So, with feelings of hopelessness and helplessness, he will develop suicidal tendencies and may believe that death is the only alternative, and one day, he may attempt suicide when he finds that there is no relief from suffering. So, a link is established between suicide and mental disorders in advanced countries, where many suicides happen impulsively in moments of crisis, because most people are unable to cope with life stresses, due to financial problems, relationship breakups, or chronic pain and illness. The prevention of suicide has not been adequately addressed due to a lack of awareness of suicide as a major public health problem in many countries.

The correlates of suicide in India are: (i) family problems, (ii) illness (including mental illness), (iii) unemployment, (iv) love affairs, (v) drug abuse and drug addiction, (vi) failure in examination, (vii) bankruptcy or debt, (viii) sudden change in economic status, (ix) poverty, and (x) dowry dispute.

METHODS USED IN SUICIDES

One of the following methods is used by the suiciders while committing suicide:

1. **Hanging:** The most common method of committing suicide is hanging. The suicide (the person who intends to die) hangs himself from the ceiling fan in his room after tying his neck with a rope or any piece of cloth while standing on a stool and then removes it. After a few minutes, he is no more because his breathing stops and his body falls unconscious.
2. **Drowning:** In this method, the suicider throws himself in the river or canal or any other place like a pool where the water is too deep to swim. This is the easiest way of committing suicide and is less painful. His body is found floating a short distance or many meters away from the place of jumping into the water.

3. **Poisoning:** Another way of committing suicide is to take in any poisonous medicine, drugs, or pesticides. These illegal medicines are available in some of the chemist shops and are saleable at higher prices.
4. **Shootings:** Sometimes, a person under depression commits suicide by firing on his forehead or any other part of the body out of rage or anger with his gun or pistol. It is only possible if he has in his possession any legal or illegal weapon at his home.
5. **Suicide at the Railway track**: Those who live near the railway station or those who have access to the railway track may think of dying before the train. They throw themselves on the railway track before the incoming of the train or pass the train on that path. This is a very painful method, and it may be that the person may be saved by a passerby, or some grievous injury may take place.
6. **Injury to the body:** Sometimes, the suicider tries to cut his veins with a knife or other weapon to show others that he does not want to live, as he is a miserable person.
7. **Putting petrol on the body:** It is common practice with ladies to throw petrol or kerosene oil on their bodies and then set themselves on fire. It is done in the kitchen, where kerosene oil is easily available.
8. **Jumping from height**: One of the common methods of committing suicide is jumping from a height from a building or some other place. In metropolitan cities like Bombay, Delhi, and Kolkata, it is often found that suiciders try to jump from the 8th or 10th story of their building or flats.

Knowledge of the most used suicide methods is important to devise effective prevention strategies. The methods of suicide in India are: (i) poisoning (31%), (ii) hanging (26%), (iii) firearms (16%), (iv) burns (11%), (v) drowning (10%), and (vi) falling from height (6%). Now it has become practice to prepare a suicide note on some pieces of paper and put it in the pockets of their pants or keep it on the table near their place of suicide. It has been seen these days that some suicidal victims have prepared a video for a few minutes before committing suicide.

WARNING SIGNS OF SUICIDE

Most suicidal individuals give warning signals of their intentions to die. They always discuss death and talk about negative things or write about life and death questions. They discuss how to harm themselves and others. They will always have some weapons or drugs that can be used to make suicide. These signals are even more acute if the person has a mental depression, or if he has previously attempted to commit suicide, or has a family history of suicide. Suiciders may also lose interest in day-to-day activities, neglect their appearance, or show big changes in their eating or sleeping habits. Warning signs of suicide may include the following:

1. **Talking about irrelevant things:** Any talk about suicide, dying, or self-harm is the first warning sign of suicidal tendency. Talking about negative things, feeling hopelessness, and helplessness is a signal that the person is thinking internally to die, as he does not want to live, and it may be that one day, he may take any drastic step.
2. **Way to find out lethal weapons:** Such a person is always trying to find out some lethal weapon, guns, pills, knives, or other objects that could be used in a suicide attempt. He may also seek the help of someone else to procure these objects illegally.
3. **Self-destructive behaviour:** Such a person has self-destructive behaviour because he has a negative attitude, feelings, and actions. So, he remains busy in abusive behaviours, including excessive alcohol or drug consumption, reckless driving, and taking unnecessary risks, as he has a wish to die earlier.
4. **No hope for the future:** Such a person doesn't see any bright future. He always sees the darkness in his life and not the red roses. He thinks that things will never get better or change. So, he wants to die instead of living.
5. **Pre-occupation with the idea of death:** The person with suicidal tendencies is always preoccupied with the thought of dying earlier. There is always an unusual focus on death, dying, or violence, and writing poems or stories about death.
6. **Withdrawal behaviour:** Such a person has withdrawal behaviour and has increased social isolation. He does not like to mix with his friends and family members and avoids social interactions with others. It is not good for mental health.
7. **Feelings of self-hatred:** Such a person develops feelings of self-loathing and self-hatred, as there are feelings of worthlessness, guilt, shame, and self-hatred, and hence thoughts about committing suicide occur in the mind.
8. **Sudden sense of calm:** A sudden sense of calm and happiness after being extremely depressed can mean that the person has decided to attempt suicide. It means that he is searching for a means of doing personal harm, such as buying a gun, etc.

You can't see what a person is feeling on the inside, so it isn't always easy to identify when someone is having suicidal thoughts.

EFFECTS OF SUICIDE IN SOCIETY

Suicide is a leading cause of death in our country and a major public health concern. When a person dies by suicide, the effects are felt by family, friends, and communities. Suicide committed by an individual has various ramifications in society. It not only affects the immediate members of society, e.g., wife, mother, sister, or daughters and sons, but also various sects of society. For example:

1. Suicide committed by someone affects the mental and emotional health of others and the community. When people die by suicide, their family and friends can experience shock, anger, guilt, and depression. Many other people are affected by knowing someone who dies by suicide or by personally experiencing suicidal thoughts.
2. People who attempt suicide and survive later may experience serious injuries, such as broken bones or brain injury. These injuries may have long-term effects on their health. People who survive suicide attempts may also experience depression and other mental health problems.
3. Socio-economic problems such as unemployment, poverty, homelessness, and discrimination may exacerbate suicidal thoughts.
4. Most people who die by suicide may have major depressive disorder or such as bipolar disorder. Other conditions implicated include schizophrenia, personality disorders, bipolar disorder, obsessive-compulsive disorder, and post-traumatic stress disorder.
5. The psychological health consequences are: (i) denial, (ii) withdrawal, and (iii) the ability to function normally in their daily lives. But the long-term psychological effects are: (i) depression and chronic anxiety, (ii) feelings of vulnerability, (iii) loss of self-esteem, (iv) emotional distress, (v) distorted sense of self, (vi) nightmares, (vii) self-blame, (viii) mistrust, (ix) avoidance, and (x) chronic mental disorders.
6. Suicidal thoughts and attempted suicide take an emotional toll. For instance, you may be so involved in suicidal thoughts that you can't function in your daily life. While many attempted suicides are impulsive acts during a moment of crisis, they can leave you with permanent severe injuries, such as organ failure or brain damage. Those who are left behind after a suicide develop feelings of grief, anger, depression, and guilt.

CAUSATIVE FACTORS OF SUICIDE

Suicides can take place due to many causes. They are the result of feelings and thoughts that you can't cope with or adjust to overwhelming life situations. When someone loses hope in a crisis for the future, he may wrongly think that suicide is the only solution. Moreover, people who commit suicide or who have suicidal thoughts are more likely to have a family history of suicide.

Stressful life events: It is said that some of the causes of suicide are stressful life events that may be due to conviction, illness, desertion by family members, debt, etc. Moreover, (i) bereavement in the family, (ii) money matters, e.g., loss in business, dismissal from the job or dejection in the professional life, (iii) unemployment or underemployment, (iv) end of relationship, divorce, or desertion, (v) loss of social support, and (vi) major life change in work may be some of the other causes of suicides. Some others commit suicide due to acute stress, which is caused by financial problems, troubles with family relationships, or job dissatisfaction. So, suicide is "the act of taking one's own life".

Stressful life events such as the loss of a family member or friend, loss of a job, legal troubles or financial problems, or social isolation increase the risk. Those who remain unmarried throughout life are also at greater risk. Being religious may reduce one's risk of suicide. Some may take their own lives to escape bullying or prejudice. The history of childhood sexual abuse and time spent in foster care are also risk factors.

Depression: Several factors can increase the risk of suicide, such as having a mental disorder. Not all people who die by suicide have a known mental illness at the time of their death. Depression is the top mental health risk factor, but others include bipolar disorder, schizophrenia, anxiety disorders, and personality disorders.

Depression is one of the causes among suicidal persons which may be due to: (i) a sad or depressed mood that may be persistent, (ii) loss of interest and enjoyment, (iii) reduced energy, fatigability, or tiredness, (iv) reduced attention and concentration, (v) reduced self-esteem and self-confidence, (vi) ideas of guilt and unworthiness, (vii) pessimistic views of future, (viii) ideas of self-harm, (ix) disturbed sleep, (x) diminished appetite, (xi) somatic symptoms, and (xii) sometimes psychotic symptoms.

Psychosocial states as risk factors: Several psychological conditions increase the risk of suicide, including hopelessness, loss of pleasure in life, depression, and anxiousness. Inability to solve problems and poor impulse control also play a role. Interpersonal stressors (such as shame, harassment, bullying, discrimination, or relationship troubles) may contribute to suicide risk factors. Egoistic suicide is when the person feels that they are not part of society, or when the elders feel that they are a burden on others.

The factors that affect the risk of suicide include psychological states, cultural, family, and social situations, and genetics. Other risk factors include having previously attempted suicide, the ready availability of a means to take one's life, a family history of suicide, or the presence of traumatic brain injury. For example, suicide rates are greater in households with firearms than in those without them.

Poverty is also associated with the risk of suicide. Over 200,000 farmers in India have died by suicide since 1997, partly due to the problem of debt. In China, suicide is three times as likely in rural regions as in urban ones, partly due to financial difficulties in that country.

Drug abuse: After major depression and bipolar disorders, drug abuse is the most common risk factor for suicide. When combined with personal grief, such as bereavement, the risk is further increased. Drug use and misuse are also associated with mental health disorders, leading to suicide.

The misuse of cocaine and methamphetamine has a high relationship with suicide. Those who used inhalants are also at significant risk of attempting suicide at some point. Smoking cigarettes is also associated with the risk of suicide, because smoking causes health problems that subsequently make people want to end their lives. Besides mental health conditions, other factors that increase the risk of suicide include substance abuse, including alcoholism and the use of benzodiazepines.

Most people who have risk factors for suicide will not attempt suicide. Although risk factors for suicide are important to keep in mind, someone who is showing *warning signs* of suicide may be at higher risk for danger and need immediate attention. The difficulty that suicidal people have in imagining a solution to their suffering is due in part to the distorted thinking caused by depression.

To sum up, it can be said that other causes of committing suicide are as follows:

1. Suicide is due to frustration in life, which leads to burnout.
2. Depression may be due to financial loss, debt, the death of a loved one, or shock.
3. Loss of self-prestige cracks in inter-personal relationships.
4. Feelings of failure and disappointment.
5. Feelings of helplessness and hopelessness.
6. Impulsive act due to stress.
7. A non-fatal suicide attempt may try again to commit suicide.
8. Post-traumatic stress disorder.

PREVENTION AND CONTROL

It is the foremost duty for psychologists, especially clinical psychologists and psychiatrists, to help society in eradicating the problem of suicide and find a permanent solution, so that no person tends to commit suicide. For the prevention of suicide, firstly, we will have to recognize the warning signs of suicide and know the causes of suicidal behaviour. If we come to know that a friend or family member is suicidal, we can play a role in suicidal prevention by discussing their problem, which may be the cause of suicide, telling them that we care, and we will get a doctor or psychologist consulted.

Suicide is a very complex and serious problem, and therefore efforts for suicide prevention and control require coordination and collaboration among multiple sectors of society, including health, education, agriculture, business, justice, law, defense, politics, and the media. Suicides can be preventable. Several measures can be taken to prevent suicide and its attempts. The following effective interventions are recommended, which may include:

(i) An attempt should be made to reduce access to the means of suicide (e.g., pesticides, firearms, poisons, and certain medications).

(ii) After early identification, treatment should be started for people with mental disorders, chronic pain, and acute emotional distress.

(iii) The state should introduce alcohol policies to reduce the harmful use of alcohol.

(iv) The state should provide training to non-specialized health workers in the assessment and management of suicidal behaviour.

(v) We should assess, manage, and follow up with anyone who is affected by suicidal behaviours.

(vi) We should follow-up care for people who have attempted suicide and provide community support.

(vii) School-based intervention programs should be made possible, e.g., inculcating socio-emotional life skills among adolescents.

(viii) The media should responsibly report the cases of suicide.

(ix) Counseling should be done for those who are under depression and have suicidal tendencies.

(x) Social and moral support is needed for those who are suffering from some mental disorder.

Some Useful Tips for Suicide Prevention

The following points should be followed if you find that somebody near you is likely to commit suicide:

1. **Talk to if somebody is worried**: If you find the warning signs and symptoms of suicide in someone you care about, or if anyone talks about suicide or shows other warning signs, he/she needs immediate attention and help. Talking to a friend or family member

about their suicidal thoughts and feelings can be helpful. Giving a suicidal person the opportunity to express their feelings can provide relief from pent-up negative emotions and may prevent a suicide attempt. By talking to that person, most of his problems would be solved.

2. **Respond quickly in a crisis:** If you find that a friend or family member tells you that he is thinking about death or suicide, it's important to assess the immediate danger the person is facing. Those who are at the highest risk of committing suicide will surely have a specific suicide plan, the method to carry out the plan, a time set for doing it, and an intention to do it. You should react and help them quickly.
3. **Offer help and support:** If a friend or family member has suicidal tendencies, the best way to help is by offering empathetic listening. Let your loved ones know that they're not alone and that you care for them too much. You can offer moral and social support, but you can't help a suicidal person get better until they have changed their mind. They must make a personal commitment to recovery if they have developed insight into their problems.
4. **Take care of yourself**: It takes a lot of courage to help someone who is suicidal. Witnessing a loved one dealing with thoughts about ending his own life can stir up many difficult emotions. As you're helping a suicidal person, don't forget to take care of yourself. Find someone that you trust, your friend, family member, or counselor, to talk to about your feelings and get support of your own.

Some other points that help the suiciders are as follows:

1. **Seek professional advice:** If the problem is not solved, or if you find that the person is adamant about committing suicide, it is better to consult a specialist or a professional expert in this case or refer the case to a psychiatrist to get advice. You may persuade the person to see a mental health professional or clinical psychologist, get a treatment facility or take him to a doctor's appointment for diagnosis.
2. **Treatment follow-up:** If the doctor prescribes medication, make sure the person takes it as directed. We should be aware of the possible side effects of the medicine and be sure to consult the doctor if the need arises. It often takes time to find the medication that's right for a particular person. If the clinical psychologist suggests some mental exercises, you should see that the person is doing these exercises daily in the morning or at any other time regularly.

3. **Be proactive:** Those who are thinking of committing suicide often believe they cannot be helped, or they do not want to be helped, so you may have to be more proactive at offering help and moral support. You should not be disheartened but feel encouraged to help him save his life. You should not wait for the person to call you.
4. **Encourage a positive lifestyle:** You may encourage that person to change his negative thoughts into positive lifestyles, such as a healthy diet, plenty of sleep, and getting out in the sun or sitting outside in nature for at least 30 minutes each day. For him, morning walk and physical exercise are also extremely important as they release endorphins, relieve stress, and promote emotional well-being.
5. **Make a safety plan:** You may help the person adhere to a set of patterns he promises to follow during the period of crisis. It will identify any trigger that may lead to a suicidal crisis, such as loss of anniversary or stress from relationships, which may also include forgetting the contact or telephone numbers for the person's doctor, as well as friends and family members who are ready to help in an emergency.
6. **Remove potential means of suicide:** It will be much better if we remove all the possible means that may help to commit suicide, e.g., such as pills, knives, razors, or firearms. If the person is likely to get an overdose of some drug, then lock up the medicines or give them only as he needs them.
7. **Continue your support for the long term:** Even after the person has undergone through immediate suicidal crisis, you should remain in touch with that person and go for a medical checkup periodically. Your social support is essential to ensure your friend or loved one remains on the recovery track.

In summary, it can be said that to help a person with suicidal tendencies, the following ten suggestions should be implemented:

1. Let the person know you care that he is not alone. Give him full hope.
2. Let your friend or loved one vent and unload his feelings. Try to listen to what he wants to say.
3. The suicidal person is doing the right thing by talking about his feelings, no matter how much patience is required to hear from him. You should be sympathetic to him.
4. You should reassure your loved one that help is available and that the suicidal feelings are temporary. Let the person know that his life is important to you. Try to make him optimistic.

5. If a suicidal person says things like, "I'm so depressed," ask if he has thoughts of suicide. In this way, you're helping him to share his pain with you.
6. You should avoid saying things like: "You have so much to live for," "Your suicide will hurt your family," etc. You should not argue but persuade him into positivity.
7. You may lecture on the value of life or argue that suicide is wrong. Say some motivating words that may help him to come out of the negative thoughts of suicide.
8. Life is at stake, and you may need to speak to a mental health professional to keep the suicidal person safe. If you promise to keep your discussions secret, you may have to convince him that the whole matter is confidential.
9. You should give advice or make him feel like they must shun their suicidal feelings and become normal human beings.
10. You can't "fix" someone else's negative thoughts on yourself. Your friend or loved one's happiness, or lack thereof, is not your liability but responsibility.

PSYCHO-MEDICAL THERAPIES FOR TREATMENT

If the prevention of suicide is not possible, or if you fail to persuade the person to take such a drastic act, then medical treatment is also available to help that individual. Suicidal thoughts do not go away on their own, so it is better to get help from a professional expert. It is better to **get the treatment the person needs.** If you don't seek treatment for mental health problems like suicide or get the right treatment at the right time, you may be too late in saving a precious life. Remember that effective interventional therapies are available to help people who are at risk of suicide: For example:

1. **Cognitive Behavioural Therapy (CBT):** CBT is a type of psychotherapy that can help people learn new ways of coping with stressful and painful experiences. It helps to recognize their thought patterns and consider alternative actions when thoughts of suicide arise. It helps to convert negative thoughts to positive ones and solve the problem.
2. **Dialectical Behaviour Therapy (DBT):** DBT is another type of psychotherapy that has been found to reduce suicidal behaviour. It helps the adults with borderline personality disorder, which is a severe mental illness leading to suicide. It is characterized by an ongoing pattern of varying moods, self-image, and behaviour that often results in impulsive actions and problems in relationships. A

therapist trained in DBT can help a person recognize his disruptive and unhealthy feelings or actions and teach him the skills that can help to deal more effectively with upsetting situations.

3. **Brief Intervention Strategies:** It is better to prepare a crisis response plan with specific instructions for what to do and how to get help when having thoughts about suicide, which can help reduce a person's risk of acting on suicidal thoughts. Staying connected and following up with people who are at risk of suicide will also prove to help reduce the risk of future suicide attempts. Moreover, all the techniques that are used to tackle depressive or mood disorders can be used in the case of suicidal people.
4. **Collaborative Care:** Collaborative care is a team-based approach to mental health care. It is a joint effort to save a person from committing suicide. A professional health care expert will work with the person, and mental health specialists will develop a treatment plan. Collaborative care is an effective way to treat and reduce the incidence of suicide cases.
5. **Anti-depressant Medicines**: Usually, antidepressant drugs are generally safe. However, it should be kept in mind that anti-depressant medications are more likely to reduce suicide risk in the long run by improving mood.

CONCLUSION

Suicide is a very serious social problem. It is a self-murder and a kind of mental disorder. Suicide is death caused by injuring oneself with the intent to die. A suicide attempt is when someone harms himself to end his life. Common methods used in suicides are hanging, pesticide poisoning, and firearms, as well as jumping into canals and rivers, and throwing oneself on the railway track before the incoming train are other methods of committing suicide. The methods of suicide in India are: (i) poisoning, (ii) hanging, (iii) firearms, (iv) burns, (v) drowning, and (vi) falling from height.

The risk factors include mental disorders such as depression, bipolar disorder, schizophrenia, personality disorders, and substance abuse, including alcoholism and the use of benzodiazepines. Other risk factors for suicide include: (i) childhood abuse, (ii) recent traumatic events, (iii) lack of a support network, (iv) availability of a gun or weapon, (v) hostile social or school environment, and (vi) exposure to other teen suicides.

Suicide is a desperate attempt to escape suffering that has become unbearable. The causes of suicide in India are: (i) family problems, (ii) mental illness, (iii) unemployment, (iv) love affairs, (v) drug abuse, and drug addiction, (vi) failure in examination, (vii) bankruptcy or debt, (viii) sudden change in economic status, (ix) poverty, and (x) dowry dispute.

Suicide is a complex issue, and therefore suicide prevention efforts require coordination and collaboration among multiple sectors of society, including health, education, agriculture, business, justice, law, defense, politics, and the media. Suicides are preventable. Several measures can be taken at the group and individual levels to prevent suicide and suicide attempts. The effective interventional therapies are available to help people who are at risk of suicide.

12

MENTAL AND EMOTIONAL HEALTH: CARE AND PROMOTION

INTRODUCTION

Mental and emotional health includes mental, emotional, psychological, and social well-being. They affect how we think, feel, act, and relate to others. Mental health is more than the absence of a mental illness, as it's essential to our psychological wellness. Self-care can play an important role in maintaining our mental and emotional health. It also helps with the treatment and recovery if we have any emotional problems. Psychologists should consider it to be their first and foremost duty to help mentally and emotionally ill people lead a normal life in society. Mental health professionals who help in solving serious personality problems and dealing with people having problems of adjustment contribute to the welfare of humanity. Perhaps this would be the greatest contribution of a psychologist to mankind.

Many emotional, psychological, or physical events can cause symptoms of mental and emotional illness. Some of the most common causes are: (i) stressful life events, such as the loss of a dear one, family conflicts, and changes in relationships, (ii) incomplete recovery after having treatment, and (iii) medical conditions, such as obesity, heart disease, and diabetes. Psychologists are trying to devise some strategies through which mentally ill persons can be helped to overcome these mental and emotional health problems. They also suggest some techniques for the maintenance, preservation, and promotion of mental and emotional health. The functions of mental health programs are threefold: (i) prevention of mental disorders, (ii) promotion of mental health, and (iii) cure and treatment for those who have been affected with some mental illness.

MENTAL HEALTH CARE

It is necessary to understand that the prevention of mental disorders should be considered at the priority level. Recent advances in the field of psychiatry have given grounds for early treatment and recovery. It has been determined that certain causes of mental illnesses are entirely controllable, and hence preventive measures should be sincerely promoted. There is a great advantage in the promotion of mental and emotional health, which may result from a better understanding of nature and the importance of mental health, and how more successful adaptations may be made.

To develop and implement mental and emotional health programs, it is essential not only to maintain and promote the psychological well-being of human beings, but also to address the needs of people with defined mental disorders. The effectiveness of key interventions for mental disorders in different countries has been found to be true. Examples of interventions that are effective and affordable include:

- Treatment of depression with psychological care and anti-depressant medicines for moderate to severe cases.
- Treatment of psychosis with antipsychotic medicines and psycho-social support.
- Restriction of alcoholic beverages of their availability and marketing.

A range of effective measures also exists for the prevention of suicide, prevention and treatment of mental disorders in children, prevention and treatment of dementia, and treatment of substance use disorders.

Self-Caring for mental and emotional health is also very important. Self-care means taking the time to do things that help us live well and improve our physical, mental, and emotional health. When it comes to mental health, self-care can help us to manage stress, lower our risk of illness, and increase our psychic energy. Even small acts of self-care in our daily lives can have a big impact. Here are some tips to help us get started with self-care:

1. **Get regular exercise:** Just 30 minutes of walking every day can help boost our mood and improve our health. We should do a small amount of physical exercise for about 15 to 20 minutes to make ourselves physically fit.
2. **Eat healthy and regular meals:** A balanced diet and plenty of water can improve our energy throughout the day. Also, we should minimize caffeinated beverages such as soft drinks or coffee.
3. **Make sleep a priority**: We should sleep for at least 6 to 8 hours daily. We should stick to our sleeping schedule and make sure that we are getting enough sound sleep.

4. **Try a relaxing activity:** We should resort to relaxation or wellness programs, which may include meditation, progressive muscle relaxation, or breathing exercises. We may plan regular times for these and other healthy and useful activities in which we enjoy our hobbies during our leisure time.
5. **Set goals and priorities:** We should set our goals according to priorities. We must decide what should be done now and what can be postponed. We may try to be mindful of what we have accomplished at the end of the day, not what we have been unable to do.
6. **Practice gratitude:** We must remind ourselves of which daily things we are grateful for. We should be specific and write them in a diary at night or imagine them in our mind.
7. **Focus on positivity**: We should identify and recognize our negative and unhelpful thoughts and try to convert them into positive ones.
8. **Stay connected:** We may reach out to our friends or family members who can provide social and emotional support and practical help.

Self-care seems to be different for everyone, and it is important to find what we need and enjoy. It may take some time to discover what works best for us. Although self-care is not a cure for mental and emotional illnesses, understanding what causes our mild symptoms and what coping techniques work for us can help maintain our mental and emotional health.

IMPROVEMENT OF MENTAL AND EMOTIONAL HEALTH

Both mental and emotional health are related to each other, and both depend upon each other. It is said that a mentally healthy person must be emotionally healthy and vice versa. According to Smith and Segal (2011), "People who are emotionally and mentally healthy have the tools for coping with difficult situations and maintaining a positive outlook, which also remain focused, flexible, and creative in bad times as well as good". So, mentally and emotionally healthy people can face the rigors of life.

It is very important to improve our mental and emotional health by developing a positive attitude and cordial relationships with others. We should have good interpersonal relationships with others. Social relationships should be developed. Another way to improve mental and emotional health is by participating in those activities that allow you to relax and enjoy yourself. Yoga is a good example of both physical and mental exercise, which calms your entire body and mind, as it is a physio-psychological activity.

For maintaining and strengthening mental and emotional health, it's important to pay attention to our own feelings. We should not provide any opportunity where stress, tension, and negative emotions build up. We should try to maintain a balance between our daily functions. If we take care of ourselves, we will be better prepared to deal with challenges and difficulties when we face them.

To improve mental and emotional health, we should keep ourselves physically fit, mentally alert, and emotionally stable, which will help us to have happier and more relaxed lifestyles. So, emotional health includes mental, emotional, and spiritual health, as it includes physical health. We should pursue those activities that naturally release endorphins and contribute to feeling good. We should practice the following things in life:

1. **Do only those things that positively impact others:** If we want to be useful to others and are considered valued for what we do, we should perform positive acts that may have a comforting effect on others. We should also build self-esteem and develop self-confidence, so that we may have a sound self-image and self-concept.
2. **Practice self-discipline:** Commitment, control, and challenge are important ingredients in the successful life of a person. These ingredients help practice self-discipline. Self-control naturally leads to a sense of hopefulness and can help us overcome despair, helplessness, and other negative thoughts. Dedication, devotion, and determination are also required in life.
3. **Discover something new**: We should try to explore something new. We should initiate innovative ideas, e.g., we should take risks to try something new. We may join a club, visit a museum, go hiking and trekking, or travel to a new place. We should discover new things and try doing some experiments. So, we should find time out of our busy lives for these activities.
4. **Enjoy the beauty of nature:** It has been proven that simply walking through a garden or going for a morning walk in a park can lower blood pressure, cholesterol and reduce stress. In the garden, you can enjoy the beauty of nature, seeing the green grass, the flow of water from fountains in the lawns, and the chirping of the birds. The same goes for strolling through a park, hiking, appreciating the natural beauty, or sitting on a beach.

For taking care of ourselves, there are many other strategies that we must follow. For example:

1. **Appeal to our senses**: We should stay calm and energized by appealing to our five senses: sight, sound, touch, smell, and taste. We should listen to music that improves our mood, see the flowers and smell them, massage our hands and feet, or sip a warm drink, either tea or coffee. In this way, you will be able to enjoy your day.

2. **Engage in meaningful and creative work:** We should do those things that tap our creativity and make us feel proud and productive. Activities like gardening, painting, writing a poem, playing an instrument, or building something new with the blocks are the ones in which we must engage ourselves.
3. **Get a pet:** If possible, you may have a pet dog. Though it is a responsibility, caring for one makes you feel honored and loved. There is no love lost that is quite as unconditional as the love a pet can give you. Dogs can also get you out of the house for a walk and expose you to new people and places.
4. **Make leisure time a priority:** Leisure time activity is essential and very much required in life. In our leisure time, we may engage ourselves in some hobby or any other useful and productive activity. We may keep ourselves busy painting a drawing, playing on a harmonium, or any other musical instrument, or listening to songs and enjoying music. We may read a good book or talk to a friend. Leisure time activity is an emotional and mental health necessity.
5. **Make time for contemplation and appreciation:** We should think about those things that we are grateful for. We should meditate, pray, enjoy the sunset, or simply take a moment to pay attention to what is good, positive, and beautiful as you go about your day.

PROMOTION OF MENTAL AND EMOTIONAL HEALTH

Mental and emotional health promotion consists of those actions that can improve psychological well-being. This may involve creating an environment that supports mental health. An environment that protects the basic civil, political, socio-economic, and cultural rights is the basis of mental and emotional health. Without the security and freedom provided by these rights, it isn't easy to maintain a high level of mental and emotional health. Mental and emotional health promotion should be mainstreamed into governmental and non-governmental policies and programs. Specific ways to promote mental and emotional health include:

1. We should provide a congenial environment that is helpful to children's health needs, and provide opportunities for early learning, and interactions that are emotionally supportive, and stimulating.
2. We should provide children with life skills and development programs.
3. Socio-economic empowerment of women is important for improving the facilities for education and other schemes.

4. Social support for elderly populations is essential, which involves taking initiatives for starting community and day centers for the aged.
5. Programs should be started for marginalized people, including minorities, migrants, and people affected by disasters. They should include psycho-social schemes for interventions after disasters and support for those affected.
6. Mental health promotional activities should be started in schools (e.g., programs involving supportive ecological changes in schools). Drill and mental exercise should be conducted off and on.
7. Mental health interventions at workplaces should be a part of their routine schedule. Stress management programs should be introduced by organizing training workshops, seminars, or inviting experts off and on.
8. Housing policies (e.g., housing improvement) should be initiated. It should be done by the state.
9. Some social organizations or non-governmental agencies should apply violence prevention programs (e.g., reducing the availability of alcohol and access to arms).
10. Community development programs should be started where integrated rural as well as urban development should be undertaken.

World Health Organization (WHO) supports the goal of strengthening and promoting mental and emotional health. The main objective is to promote mental and emotional well-being, prevent mental disorders, provide care, enhance recovery, promote human rights, and disability for people with mental disorders. It focuses on four key objectives, too:

(i) To strengthen effective leadership and governance for mental health.
(ii) To provide comprehensive, integrated, responsive mental and emotional health and social care services in community-based settings.
(iii) To implement strategies for promotion and prevention in mental and emotional health.
(iv) To disseminate information, evidence, and research for mental and emotional health.

PROMOTION OF MENTAL AND EMOTIONAL HEALTH THROUGH PHYSICAL ACTIVITIES

Psychologists and behavioural scientists have advocated the idea that physical activities help to improve the mental and emotional health of human beings. They also promote healthy emotional functioning and the acquisition of acceptable social values. In this age, physical activities are assuming increasing importance in modern society. Physical educators are devising some forms of physical exercise that may contribute to increasing human happiness and improving social adjustment. The following factors will help promote mental and emotional health:

1. There is a close relationship between body and mind, which has led to a bond between physical health and mental and emotional health that leads to adequate social adjustment. Physical exercises contribute positively to the maintenance of physical health, which will help in promoting good mental and emotional health.
2. Physical illness and mental disorders are interrelated, as physical diseases lead to mental illnesses. Diagnosis, understanding, or treatment of both physical and mental illnesses is not possible unless they are viewed as both organic and psychological problems. It has been observed that organic illness may cause emotional problems, and that psycho-somatic disorders require both medical and psychological treatment. Hence, poor physical fitness may be related to poor mental health.
3. The physical activities help promote mental and emotional health and prevent delinquency. Participation in physical activities in school tends to be associated with good emotional and social adjustment. The programs of supervised play can reduce the occurrence of delinquent behaviour.
4. When physical activities, games, and other co-curricular activities are planned with individual needs in mind, they may be very useful means of improving mental and emotional health as well as social adjustment. Principles of play therapy could be applied in physical education programs of schools and educational institutions.
5. Physical exercises and sports activities channelize the surplus energies of adolescents, as they supply outlets for the expression of emotions, and it has been claimed by psychologists that the expressions of emotions in approved activities tend to provide release from stress and promote mental health. Recently, psychiatrists have pointed out that the expression of hostile aggression may even generate feelings of guilt as well as increase tensions. Only sports provide the opportunity to express your aggressive tendencies in games like boxing and wrestling, etc., in socially approved ways.
6. Psychiatrists have indicated that outward expression of emotion is very much needed, as that expression of negative feelings does not increase feelings of guilt, but it can lead to self-acceptance, self-understanding, and free communication. The value of expressing positive feelings through games and physical activities is acceptable.

7. Physical activities may enhance social development and the acquisition of desirable personality traits. For many individuals, sports competitions tend to favor the development of positive personality traits. When individuals are encouraged to participate in activities in which they have some chance for success, co-operation, loyalty, and sportsmanship, it means that we are helping them to promote their mental and emotional health.
8. The physical education teacher can get valuable information regarding the various mental health problems of children or youth. Consequently, he can provide information that contributes significantly to the diagnosis of a therapeutic program.
9. Physical education activities provide a favorable environment for the development of social, moral values, and socially acceptable character traits. It is necessary to emphasize the desirability of sportsman spirit, fair play, honesty, cooperation, teamwork, tolerance, and other so-called character traits and to encourage their development.

EFFECT OF EXERCISE ON MENTAL AND EMOTIONAL HEALTH

The National Institute of Mental Health discussed the possibilities and limitations of physical activity for coping with stress and depression (Morgan & Goldston, 1987). In terms of the effect of exercise on mental-emotional health, the panel concluded the following:

1. Physical fitness is positively associated with mental health and emotional well-being.
2. Exercise is associated with the reduction of emotional states like state anxiety.
3. Anxiety and depression are common symptoms of failure to cope with mental stress, and physical exercise has been associated with a decreased level of mild to moderate depression and anxiety.
4. Physical exercise is also associated with a reduction in traits such as neuroticism and anxiety.
5. Severe depression usually requires professional treatment, which may include physical exercise, medication, electroconvulsive therapy, psychotherapy, or a combination of these.
6. Appropriate physical exercise results in reductions in various stress indicators, such as neuromuscular tension, resting heart rate, and some stress hormones.
7. Current clinical opinion holds that physical exercise has beneficial emotional effects across ages and genders.
8. Physically healthy people who require psychotropic medication may safely exercise under close medical supervision.

EFFECT OF DIET AND NUTRITION ON MENTAL AND EMOTIONAL HEALTH

Research has found that dietary patterns may have a positive effect on mental and emotional health. Most studies have focused on the effects of the standard Western diet. Many studies have found that women who eat unhealthy Western diets have more psychological problems. Those who are eating processed foods, fried foods, and refined grains, such as white bread, sugary products, and beer, are likely to develop mental and emotional illnesses. Similar unhealthful dietary patterns lead to obesity, diabetes, and other physical health problems and can also contribute to poor mental and emotional health.

On the other hand, people who follow a simple diet seem to be less likely to have mental and emotional health problems. So, it has been suggested that a healthy diet can improve mental and emotional health and help treat or prevent certain psychological problems. We have also found out how food affects our health and how a nutritious diet affects our mental and emotional health.

Usually, the Indian diet consists of : (i) plenty of fruits and vegetables, (ii) whole grains, (iii) potatoes, (iv) cereals, (v) beans and pulses, (vi) nuts and seeds, (vii) olive oil, (viii) low-to-moderate amounts of dairy products, fish, and poultry, (ix) very little red meat, (x) eggs up to four times a week, and (xi) low-to-moderate amounts of wine in some cases. It has been found that the relationship between food intake and mental health involves a 30–40% decrease in calorie intake while retaining protein, vitamins, minerals, and water intake to maintain proper nutrition.

There is some evidence to prove that fasting on some days or missing a meal once a week can help improve mood and mental and emotional wellness. Experts have noted that fasting could contribute to improvements in mood, as well as people's subjective sense of well-being, alertness, tranquility, and, in some cases, euphoria. Calorie restriction and fasting may also affect a person's mental and emotional health.

An Indian diet is a healthy one that can positively affect a person's weight, blood pressure, cholesterol, and other measures of health. While a healthy diet may help in the treatment of poor mental and emotional health, anyone experiencing the symptoms of a mental and emotional health problem may consult a physician or a professional.

SUGGESTIONS FOR MAINTAINING MENTAL AND EMOTIONAL HEALTH

Health maintenance, prevention of mental illness, and improving the quality of life are primary goals to be actively sought by all of us. The following are the guidelines about matters of mental and emotional health:

1. We should try to find out the causes of our behaviour during the present and past situations.
2. We should compare our thoughts, feelings, and actions with those of others and make a correct and objective assessment to arrive at a logical conclusion.
3. We may have a few very close friends with whom we can share our feelings, worries, joys, and sorrows.
4. We should show respect to others and accept love from them. Love is a reciprocal, and it is not a one-way traffic.
5. We should not say bad things about ourselves. We should not think of negative traits such as stupid, ugly, non-creative, or incorrigible, etc.
6. We should make constructive criticism about ourselves. We should analyze ourselves objectively.
7. We should always share positive feelings and thoughts with others.
8. We should take full credit for our success and happiness. We should feel proud of ourselves.
9. We should know the sources of personal strengths and weaknesses. We should also be aware of limitations.
10. When we feel that we cannot control our emotions, try to keep ourselves away from the situation or talk to someone who sympathizes with us.
11. We should not regret our past misfortunes or sources of guilt, shame, or failure. The past is past and gone and only think about our future and plan accordingly.
12. We should try to learn from our failures. We should remember that failure and disappointment are sometimes blessings in disguise.
13. 'Know thyself' should be our guideline. We should try to understand our total behaviour, which consists of cognitive, affective, and conative domains, meaning thereby thinking, feeling, and actions.
14. If we see someone acting strangely, then try to intervene in a concerned and gentle way to find out if anything is wrong and how we can help him.
15. If we find that we cannot help ourselves or another person in distress, seek the advice of a counselor or trained specialist.
16. If it is not a medical problem, we should consult a psychologist or a clinical psychologist, or a psychiatrist.
17. We should set long-range goals in life. Goal setting is very important. It is a motivating factor.
18. We should take time to relax, meditate, and enjoy hobbies and activities that we can do alone.

19. We should think of ourselves not as a passive object, but as an active agent who at any time can change the direction of our entire life.
20. If there is life, there is hope that we can achieve something in life and achieve success and pleasure. We should remember that 'Life is hope and hope is life'.

In the end, it can be said that we can affect our mental-emotional health by taking steps to improve it, such as doing meditation, using relaxation techniques, and practicing yoga. Over time, our mental health can change. For example, we may be dealing with a difficult situation, such as trying to manage a chronic illness, taking care of an ill relative, or facing money problems. The situation may wear us out and overwhelm our ability to cope with it. This can worsen our mental health. On the other hand, getting therapy may improve our mental and emotional health.

DEVELOPING A HEALTHY LIFESTYLE

People who live a long life indicate that they have a healthy lifestyle. Many factors may play a big role in their extended life spans. Physical activity is perhaps the most important factor contributing to longevity and good health among long-lived people. Regular physical exercise is an integral part of their lives, continuing well into old age. Yoga asanas keep them physically fit and mentally alert. Additional factors that may contribute to their long life span are continued sexual activity and harmonious involvement in family and community affairs during advanced years.

It is now a well-known fact that regular and vigorous exercise can significantly reduce coronary heart disease, even in the presence of other health risk factors, including high blood pressure and high blood cholesterol. Even less vigorous forms of activity can benefit if done consistently. For example, people who walk regularly for half an hour daily have fewer problems with their health. It has also been proven that exercise can have a significant impact on our mental health, e.g., exercise has been found to improve self-image and self-concept, lessen feelings of depression, and reduce anxiety. Improvement in mood following exercise may result from socializing with a friend because of the companionship that the exercise provides. Hence, it can be said that regular and vigorous exercise promotes both physical and psychological health and may develop emotional well-being.

Another factor is their diet pattern, which consists of an average consumption of grains, green vegetables, fresh milk, and fresh fruits. They tend to eat low to moderate levels of meat and maintain moderate levels of daily caloric intake. They consume no or a very small amount of alcohol or liquor. But the most important factor in their life is emotional well-being.

While genetic factors certainly play a role in determining life span, it is suggested that people may be able to extend their lives significantly by developing a lifestyle that includes factors like a balanced, low-fat diet, regular exercise, and continued activity during later years. More important than these factors is to lead a stress-free life, which is possible only if a person has few desires, fewer needs, and fewer psychological problems that can be solved rationally.

Many psychologists have recommended that mental health and emotional well-being are based on preventive strategies, i.e., techniques designed to reduce the occurrence of mental illness and other physical and psychological problems. A primary preventive strategy aims to reduce or eliminate the incidence of illness and injury. These strategies usually involve: (i) educating people about the relationship between their behaviour and their mental health, (ii) teaching motivational skills to practice healthy emotional behaviour, and (iii) directly changing poor health practices through an intervention program.

The secondary prevention strategy emphasizes early detection to decrease the severity of illness that is already present. Thus, individuals come to know about their health status through medical tests that diagnose the presence of any disease. Psychologists are taking an increasing interest in developing motivational strategies for early detection procedures, i.e., techniques used to screen for the presence of high blood pressure, high blood cholesterol, and some other forms of disorders. The identification of these conditions at an early stage is very important to start the proper treatment.

Another important factor of preventive strategy is the educational process, which is done through mass media, i.e., television programs, newspaper articles, magazine writings, and radio programs, etc., to aware us about unhealthy behaviour like smoking, alcohol, drug abuse, and unprotected sex and the risks involved, including heart disease, cancer, and AIDS. They provide information about symptoms of a health problem, such as breathlessness or chest pain in the case of heart attacks. It is observed that media, especially newspapers, can produce widespread changes in behaviour, and hence, it can be a very effective tool for promoting behavioural modification and developing a healthier lifestyle.

Advantages of a Healthy Lifestyle: Now the question arises as to why it is important to have good physical, mental, and emotional health care. The answer can be found from the following points:

1. **Psychic-energy:** We should do regular physical exercises along with a morning walk to maintain positive and healthy physical health to sustain our energy levels. Continued regular exercise and keeping a positive attitude are a must to maintain our energy levels, both physical and psychological. Emotional wellness means that

we feel energetic and healthy, relaxed, worry less, and are mentally tension-free, rather than heavy, lethargic, and fatigued physically. It will also maintain our mental health. It is only possible if we have a healthy lifestyle.

2. **Anti-aging:** Everybody feels the aging factor with signs and symptoms of early hair loss, memory loss, digestive problems, etc. But leading an emotionally healthy and well-being life will delay our aging factor. We will not feel old so early in our lives. On the other hand, a healthy and balanced lifestyle keeps us young. In fact, the impact of long-term stress affects our body adversely, due to psychosomatic problems. Maintaining a wellness lifestyle is the perfect anti-aging technique.
3. **Health**: A healthy lifestyle builds our body physically and keeps our immune system functioning normally. We are at less risk of illness and disease, which may include cardiovascular disorders and cancer. An emotional well-being lifestyle will keep us healthy.
4. **Unbiased Mind**: An emotionally well-being person who is leading a healthy and happy life, will have a poise and unbiased mind to perceive the environment independently. In this way, he will have a positive attitude in life and may be able to accomplish his daily tasks and achieve his goals easily. When we are leading a healthy lifestyle full of happiness, we have in our mind the objective to complete our routine work. Then we will feel less tense about situations and handle them with ease.
5. **Reducing Stress, Headaches and Migraines:** When we are under stress and strain, which creates anxiety, it puts a lot of pressure on our body and mind. But when we are leading a healthy lifestyle that promotes emotional wellness, headaches may become a thing of the past, and migraine attacks may not occur. Similarly, minor physical disorders like backache may be controlled, which may occasionally occur.

CHANGE YOUR HABITS AND CHANGE YOUR LIFE

Wellness is a dynamic, ever-changing, fluctuating process (Ardell 1999). It is a lifestyle, which is a kind of life, living in a way that helps you to become the best person according to your potential and abilities. You are the product of your heredity and environment. The past is history; the present is the conditions you are facing these days, and the future is the days ahead, which is based on the choices you make today. You should hope that you will *become the best kind of person you can be.*

The various concepts of wellness may include the following precepts:

1. **Wellness:** Your psychological well-being is the result of the constant interaction between the genetic factors and the circumstances in your life, i.e., nature and nurture. It is between the several natural dimensions of life and wellness. The intention is to be aware of yourself as a complete person, and to live life as fully as possible.
2. **Balance:** Due to the constantly changing nature of your life, you may try to balance the changing circumstances by paying attention to each of the dimensions. An unbalanced life may lead to unhappiness and misery. It may also cause the wrong development of your various faculties.
3. **Self-Responsibility:** A fully developed person becomes responsible for his health and happiness. He makes decisions about his future life and makes choices of his own. Self-responsibility includes self-awareness, including the process by which one becomes increasingly more aware of both the causes and consequences of his behaviour.
4. **Positive and Proactive:** Psychological well-being and wellness require primarily positive thinking, ideals, and values by which to live a healthy life. It also requires a strong sense of honesty of purpose, and quick action. These are our main presumptions, and they have stood well enough through time. However, they provide merely a simple framework.

CONCLUSION

The solution of both mental and emotional health programs includes both care as well as promotion of mental and emotional health. First, we must try to prevent mental disorders, and secondly, we must use techniques for the promotion of mental and emotional health. Self-care can play a role in maintaining our mental and emotional health and help to support our treatment and recovery program if we have developed a mental disorder and emotional difficulties. Self-care means finding the time to do things that help us live well and improve both our physical health and mental-emotional health. When it comes to our mental health, self-care can help us manage stress, control negative emotions, lower the risk of illness, and increase our energy. Taking care of ourselves includes pursuing activities that naturally release endorphins and contribute to feeling good.

Mental and emotional health promotion involves an action plan that improves psychological well-being and mental wellness. This may involve creating an environment that supports mental and emotional health. An environment that respects and protects basic civil, political, socio-economic, and cultural rights is fundamental to mental and emotional health. Physical educators think of some forms of physical exercise as making important contributions towards increasing human happiness, improving social adjustment, and directly or indirectly helping in the promotion of mental-emotional health. Psychologists have advanced many suggestions for maintaining mental and emotional health.

REFERENCES

Advance Twentieth Century Dictionary (1995), New Delhi: Educational Publishing House.

Advanced Learners Dictionary of Education (2000), New Delhi: Anmol Publishing House.

American Association of Health, Physical Education, and Recreation, (1963), *Journal of Health, Physical Education and Recreation*, Vol. 39, Issue 6.

American Psychological Association (2012), APA Washington, D.C., USA.

Ardell DB. (1999), Definition of Wellness, *Ardell Wellness Report*, 18:1–5.

Argyle, M. (2001), The Psychology of Happiness, Taylor & Francis: New York.

Argyle M. and Hills P. (2005), The Oxford Happiness Questionnaire: *Personality and Individual Differences*, 33, pp. 1073–1082.

Bandura, A. (1977), "Self-efficacy: Toward a Unifying Theory of Behavioral Change", Psychological Review, 84, pp. 191–215.

Barbara Kozier (2008), *Fundamentals of Nursing: Concepts, Process, and Practice*, Pearson Education, p. 181.

Barrow, H.M. (1977), Man, and Movement: Principles of Physical Education, Philadelphia, Lea & Fibiger, pp. 151–53.

Campbell, A.P.E. and Rodgers, W.L. (1976), The Quality of American Life: Perceptions, Evaluations, and Satisfactions, New York, Russel Sage Foundation.

Cantor, N., and Kihlstrom, J.F. (1987), Personality and Social Intelligence, Englewood Cliffs, N.J. Prentice-Hall.

Clifford Beers Clinic (2006), *About Clifford Beers Clinic*, Retrieved June 1, 2007, from CliffordBeers.org.

Clifton, D., and Rath, T. (2005), Every moment matters: how full is your bucket? Positive strategies for work and life, Gallup Press, New York, pp. 47–51.

Coleman, James, C. (1981), Abnormal Psychology and Modern Life, Pearson Scott Foresman, New York.

Compton, William C. (2005), *An Introduction to Positive Psychology,* Wadsworth Publishing pp. 1–22.

Crow and Crow (1962), Child Development and Adjustment, New York MacMillan Co.

Diagnostic and Statistical Manual of Mental Disorders-IV (DSM-IV) (1994), American Psychiatric Associatio, American Psychiatric Press, Washington, D.C.

Dictionary of Psychology (2001), Great Clarendon Street: Oxford University Press.

Diener, E. (1984), Subjective Wellbeing, Psychological Bulletin, 95, pp. 542–575.

Diener, E, and Diener, M. (1995), Cross-cultural correlates of life satisfaction and self-esteem, *Journal of Personality and Social Psychology,* 68, pp. 653–663.

Diener, E, E.M. Suh, R.E. Lucas and H.L. Smith (1999), Subjective Wellbeing—Three Decades of Progress, Psychological Bulletin.

European Psychiatric Association (2011), Strasbourg, France.

Fredrick, B.L., and Thomson, J. (2002), "Positive Emotions Trigger Upward Spirals toward Emotional Well-Being", *Psychological Science* **13** (2).

Frost, R.B. (1971), Psychological Concepts Applied to Physical Education and Coaching, Springfield, Massachusetts, Addison Wesley Pub. Co. Inc.

Goleman, D. (1995), Emotional Intelligence, Bantam Books, New York.

Goleman, D. (1995), Emotional Intelligence: "Why it can matter more than IQ", New York: Bantam Books.

Goleman, D. (1999), Working with emotional intelligence, New York: Bantam Books.

Gregory, Derek Johnston, Ron; Pratt, Geraldine et al. Eds. (June 2009), "Quality of Life", *Dictionary of Human Geography* (5th ed.), Oxford: Wiley-Blackwell.

Guilford, J. (1966), The Nature of Human Intelligence: New York, McGraw-Hill.

Harvard Health Publication (2010), "Emotional Well Being & Mental Health", Harvard Medical School, Harvard University.

Hawe, P., and Shiell, A. (2000), "Social Capital and Health Promotion: A Review," *Social Science and Medicine,* 51:871 885.

Humphrey, N. (1976), The Social functions of intellect, In P.P.G. Bateson and R.A. Hinde (Eds.), Growing points in ethnology, pp. 303–317, Cambridge, U.K. Cambridge University Press.

Humphreys, L.G. (1971), Theory of Intelligence, In R. Cancro (Ed.), Intelligence: Genetic and Environmental Influence, (31–55), New York: Grune and Stratton.

Jersild, A.T. (1968), The Psychology of Adolescence, Toronto, The MacMillan Company.

Kahneman, Daniel, and Angus Deaton (2010), "High income improves evaluation of life but not emotional well-being", *Proceedings of the National Academy of Sciences* **107** (38): 16489–16493.

Kitchener, B.A. and Joram, A.F. (2002), Mental Health First Aide Manual, Centre for Mental Health Research, Canberra, p. 5.

Layard, Richard (2006), *Happiness: Lessons from a New Science*, London: Penguin.

Longman's Dictionary of Psychology and Psychiatry (1984), Longman Inc.

Mayer, J.D. and Salovey, P. (1993), The Intelligence of Emotional Intelligence", *Intelligence,* 17, pp. 433–442.

Mayer, J.D., Caruso, D., and Salovey, P. (1999), Emotional Intelligence meets traditional standards for intelligence, *Intelligence*, 27, pp. 267–98.

Morgan, W.P., and Goldston, S.E. (1987), Exercise and mental health, Washington, DC: Hemisphere.

Murray, H. A. (2004), *Explorations in personality*, New York: Oxford University Press.

Myers, J.E., Sweeny, T.J., and Witmer, J.M. (2000), "The wheel of wellness counseling for wellness: A holistic model for treatment planning", *Journal of Counseling and Development* 78: pp. 251–266.

Page, J. D. (1976), Abnormal Psychology, New York, McGraw-Hill Publication.

Patel, V., and Prince, M. (2010), Global mental health—A new global health field comes of age, *JAMA, 303*.

Richard Layard (2006), *Happiness: Lessons from a New Science*, London: Penguin.

Richards, K.C., Campania, C., and Muse-Burke, J.L. (2010), "Self-care and Well-being in Mental Health Professionals: The Mediating Effects of Self-awareness and Mindfulness", *Journal of Mental Health Counseling*, **32** (3): 247.

Rogers, C. (1961), *On becoming a person,* Boston: Houghton Mifflin.

Rogers, C. R. (1951), "Client-Centered Therapy: Its Current Practice, Implications, and Theory", Boston: Houghton Mifflin.

Rushall, B.S. (1972), Three studies related to personality variables to football performance, *International Journal of Sport Psychology*, 3: pp. 12–24.

Ryff Carol (1995), Scales of Psychological Well-Being, University of Wisconsin, Institute on Aging, 2245 Medical Science Center, 1300 University Avenue, Madison, WI. 53706.

Ryff, C. (1989), Happiness is everything, or is it? Explorations on the meaning of psychological well-being, *Journal of Personality and Social Psychology,* 57, pp. 1069–1081.

Ryff, C., and Keyes, C. (1995), The structure of psychological well-being revisited, *Journal of Personality and Social Psychology, 69,* pp. 719–727.

Salovey, P. and Mayer, J. (1990), Emotional Intelligence, Imagination, Cognition, and Personality. 9: 185–211, Cited in Singh, D. (2002), Emotional Intelligence at Work: A Professional Guide, pp. 28–29, Sage Publications, New Delhi.

Seligman (1991), Learned optimism, New York: Knopf.

Seligman, M. E P, Steen, T., Park, N., and Peterson, C. (2005), Positive psychology progress: Empirical validation of interventions, American Psychologist, 60(5), pp. 41–421.

Sharp, Tim. (2011), "The primacy of positivity: Applications in a coaching context", Coaching: *An International Journal of Theory, Research and Practice* Vol. 4, No. 1, London.

Shenk, J. (2009), Finding happiness after Harvard, Wilson Quarterly, 33, pp. 73–74.

Strine, T.W., Chapman, D.P., Balluz, L., and Mokdad, A.H. (2008), A systematic review: Students with mental health problems a growing problem", *International Journal of Nursing Practice* 16 (1): pp. 1–6.

Thorndike, E.L. (1920), The Measurement of Intelligence, New York: Teachers College, Columbia University.

Vedantam, Shankar (2008), "Older Americans May Be Happier Than Younger Ones", The Washington Post.

Verma, S.K. (1988), Measurement of positive mental health: Some theoretical and practical considerations, *Indian Journal of Clinical Psychology,* 15, pp. 6–11.

Verma, S.K.; Dubey, B.L. and Gupta, D. (1983), P.G.I. General Wellbeing Scale—Some correlates, *Indian Journal of Clinical Psychology,* 10, pp. 299–304.

Vialle Wilma, Graduate School of Education, University of Wollongong, Australia

Wallis, Claudia (2005), "Science of Happiness: New Research on Mood, Satisfaction", TIME.

Weare, Katherine (2000), *Promoting Mental, Emotional, and Social Health: A Whole-School Approach,* London: Routledge Falmer, p. 12.

World Health Organization (2005), Promoting Mental Health: Concepts, Emerging evidence, Practice: A report of the World Health Organization, Department of Mental Health and Substance Abuse in collaboration with the Victorian Health Promotion Foundation and the University of Melbourne, World Health Organization, Geneva.

World Health Report (2001), Mental Health: New Understanding, New Hope, World Health Organization, Geneva.

World Health Report (2004), Published by the World Health Organization (WHO).

Index